In Sickness and in Health

A Story of Love in the Shadow of AIDS

Shireen Perry

with Gregg Lewis

INTERVARSITY PRESS
DOWNERS GROVE, ILLINOIS 60515

InterVarsity Press is the book-publishing division of InterVarsity Christian Fellowship, a student movement active on campus at hundreds of universities, colleges and schools of nursing. For information about local and regional activities, write Public Relations Dept., InterVarsity Christian Fellowship, 6400 Schroeder Rd., P.O. Box 7895, Madison, WI 53707-7895.

Distributed in Canada through InterVarsity Press, 860 Denison St., Unit 3, Markham, Ontario L3R 4H1, Canada.

All Scripture quotations, unless otherwise indicated, are from the Holy Bible, New International Version. Copyright © 1973, 1978, International Bible Society. Used by permission of Zondervan Bible Publishers.

Cover calligraphy: Victoria Hoke Lane
Front cover photograph: Ron Meagher
Back cover photograph: Marybeth Adkins

ISBN 0-8308-1712-3
Library of Congress Catalog Card Number: 89-15356

Printed in the United States of America ∞

17 16   15   14   13   12   11   10   9   8   7   6   5   4   3   2   1
99 98   97   96   95   94   93   92   91   90   89

Dedication

Lovingly dedicated to the memory
of my husband, Mark;
for our life together as best friends,
as companions, as spiritual partners
and as lovers;
and to those family and friends
whose love and loyalty
sustained us through our trial.

Acknowledgments

My deepest, heartfelt thanks go to my family
and friends who have shared emotional
and spiritual support in the course of this
book's creation and throughout my grieving
process. I especially appreciate the courageous
and compassionate love of Mike and Donna
Ryan and Lucy Ogden, who set the example
for the church family to respond so
supportively in our time of trial. I am also
thankful for the help of the hospice program
and Maria Swafford, the nurse who
attended to Mark. And finally, this book,
a dream of Mark's, would not have been
written without the sensitive support and help
of Gregg and Don.

This story is told primarily from Shireen's point of view. Occasionally, portions of the story, indicated by smaller type and a side rule, are told from the perspective of a third-person narrator.

CHAPTER ONE

I *WOULDN'T CALL IT LOVE AT FIRST*
sight. But the very first time I laid eyes on Mark Perry, on the
back of his head actually, I did feel a curious attraction, a definite interest. That was early December 1982.

He sat just two short rows ahead of me in a seminar at a
church-sponsored conference on Christianity and the arts. I
wasn't registered for the entire conference. I'd only had a couple hours to spare in an extremely pressured weekend. But this
Berkeley church wasn't far from home, and the conference
sounded interesting, so I made time to take in two short, Sat-
urday-morning sessions. This first seminar took place in a
bright airy room with a huge bank of windows and a gray, stone
floor.

And there he was. I didn't know his name. I'd never seen him before. But I noticed the back of his head right away. He had short, dark hair, neatly and precisely cut just above the shawl collar of a golden-brown and burgundy sweater. When he leaned over to say something to the man sitting next to him, I glimpsed just enough of a profile to note a dark, trim mustache. Everything about him added up to a perfect illustration of the word "impeccable."

Off and on throughout the session, my eyes and my mind returned to this striking man in front of me. *I wonder who he is.* And a little later, *He looks like an interesting person to meet.* And eventually, *I wonder what seminar he's going to next. Maybe I can meet him.* But I wasn't sure how to manage it. It wasn't my style to march up and introduce myself to handsome strangers.

The seminar ended, and everyone stood to take a ten-minute break before the next session. While edging my way to the aisle, I struck up a conversation with the woman who'd been sitting beside me. We chatted politely for a couple minutes before she said good-by and turned to leave. At the very same instant, the person who'd been talking with my interesting stranger walked away from him, and the two of us were left standing, not three feet apart.

"Hello," he said, extending his hand and giving me a warm smile. "I'm Mark Perry."

"Shireen Irvine," I replied, returning his smile. He wasn't tall, about 5′ 7″—almost a head taller than my 4′ 11½″. His golden-brown sweater perfectly matched one of the colors of brown in his eyes. Up close, he still had the meticulous, professional look I'd noticed from a distance.

We spent the next few minutes casually talking. He asked what had brought me to the conference. I said I enjoyed the arts and had a special interest in fabric design and floral arrangement. But that I wasn't an artist. I explained my field was home ec and I taught adaptive living skills at the state of California's Orientation Center for the Blind in nearby Albany. There had been some talk lately about possible layoffs at my school.

"If that happens, one of the fields I'd consider going into is floral design," I told Mark.

Mark said he lived in San Francisco where he had his own small business—in design and interior architecture. And he told me a little about that. He also said he'd worked for a while doing custom arrangements for a high-society florist over in San Francisco. "I know a little about the floral design field," he said. "So if you would want to get together and discuss the possibilities sometime, I'd be glad to talk to you."

"I'd love that!" I said matter-of-factly—my words more reserved than my feelings. I realized I was even more intrigued by this walking, talking, smiling Mark Perry than I had been by the back of his head. He seemed warm, cheerful, outgoing . . . but unfortunately, the next seminar was about to start.

"Then let me give you my number," he said, pulling out a card. We quickly exchanged phone numbers, and it was time to part. He reached out to shake hands again, and at that brief touch I felt something I can only describe as electricity go all the way through me.

I realized it was silly; but I practically floated home. The entire drive I couldn't get Mark off my mind. Even at first meeting I'd sensed his gentle, warm spirit. We seemed to have so much in common. Maybe a friendship could develop! I could only wish!

When I walked in the front door of my parents' house, where

I lived, my younger sister Ronah and her husband, Barry, were sitting in the living room. "What happened to you?" Ronah asked.

I knew my excitement showed.

"Ronah! I met the most wonderful man this morning! His name is Mark Perry."

"Look at her!" my brother-in-law teased. "Shireen's got sparks in her eyes. Who is this guy? Maybe we should call him Mark the Spark!"

I was too excited to mind Barry's good-natured teasing. And too excited to concentrate on my review for the final exam I'd planned to study for the rest of the day.

That night I wrote in my daily diary/prayer journal about Mark: "His whole character came across as sensitive and intuitive. . . . The experience of meeting Mark and my feelings of excitement were so strong that to get control of the almost jittery excitement, I jumped on the trampoline."

But the feelings didn't go away. They remained strong enough that a few days later I overcame my natural shyness and called Mark. I told him I would be over in the city the following day, registering for next term's graduate classes at San Francisco State University. And I wanted to take him up on his offer to talk more about the floral-design business if he'd be free for lunch. He agreed.

That night I wrote in my journal: "Thanks, Lord, for the opportunity to meet with Mark Perry tomorrow. I'm really ecstatic. Please help me to stay even-keeled, because I know this meeting may be all the time we ever spend together. Though if he's the type of person you have in mind for me, then I hope something will come about from this friendship."

The next night I wrote: "Lord, thanks for such an enjoyable

lunch with Mark Perry. Something about his spirit attracts and excites me. Though he's not the most handsome guy—dark straight hair, brown eyes, not the blue-eyed blond I always imagine. . . . He said he'd be in touch and would like to talk more. I noticed his parting handshake lingered.

"Strange, but I'm almost ready to admit he's the one I'd enjoy being a team with. That may be jumping the gun. But I already sense he's better for me than any other man I've ever met."

Days passed. Then a week. He didn't call.

My youngest sister, Marguerite, decided to help. She offered to call Mark and ask him about having a consultation with him about some remodeling her fiance was considering for his house.

Mark told Marguerite he was going to visit his brother in Fresno for Christmas. But he planned to be over in the East Bay on business one day the week after Christmas and would be glad to consult with her. He also told her he'd been thinking he'd call me and see if I could meet him for lunch that day.

When Marguerite phoned me to report on her conversation with Mark, I was thrilled. In fact, I was so excited that instead of counting the days to Christmas, I counted the days until my next lunch with Mark Perry.

He did call as soon as he got back from Fresno to ask if I could meet him for lunch a couple days later—somewhere in Oakland. I invited him to have lunch at my home instead, and he accepted.

The day finally came. And once again our time together went great. That evening my journal entry read: "Thanks for today, Lord. I really get excited about Mark. Help me to be level-headed about him. I can really understand now what it means when people say they're in a 'tizzy.' "

These strong, crazy, head-over-heels feelings I was having were a new phenomenon for me. I pride myself on being a cautious, rational person who keeps her feelings and her thoughts in careful balance. So while I can't say I didn't enjoy these surprisingly strong emotions I was experiencing, I also found them unsettling. They made me wary; I'd been badly hurt once and I didn't want to be hurt again.

Eight years before I'd been engaged to be married. I'd prayed about my decision, and I'd felt certain I'd found the man God wanted me to marry. I loved Andrew very much. Enough to want to spend the rest of my life with him.

Just four months after we got engaged (three months after we held a big open house to announce our plans to our friends), Andrew came to me and asked for his ring back. He said it just wouldn't have worked. He'd been struggling over his homosexuality and his faith for some time, and he'd finally decided to break off our engagement and give the gay lifestyle a try.

I was emotionally devastated. I felt rejected. And I became very angry. Not so much at Andrew, but at God. I'd prayed so sincerely that he'd guide me in my relationship with Andrew, and I'd felt so certain Andrew was the man I was to marry. How could I ever count on him again to guide me in my relationships with men?

I didn't admit this anger to myself, let alone anyone else, for a long time. I went to church just as I always had. I prayed. (I even prayed for Andrew.) I prayed for God's guidance in decisions regarding my health, my career, and all the other areas of my life—except one. When it came to relationships with men, my attitude was: *I can certainly handle that better myself, thank you.*

However, the truth was I didn't really trust myself any more than I trusted God. So for seven years there hadn't been another serious relationship. I'd watched my younger sister and a score of my friends get married. But I hadn't even dated much. I just hadn't let myself care or feel for anyone else what I'd felt for Andrew. It hadn't been until the summer of 1982 that my feelings began to change. It wasn't until then, with the help of counseling, that I'd recognized and let go of my anger at God and had surrendered the last of my hopes for Andrew. It was just that fall I'd begun casually dating a couple of different men.

So the intensity of my feelings for Mark, while certainly exciting, disconcerted me. And my prayers for and about him were fueled by a fresh, growing faith that maybe I could finally trust God to guide me and protect me from another hurt like I'd experienced in the past.

I invited Mark to a party at my house in January. I didn't tell him it was my birthday party because I didn't want him to feel obligated to buy me a gift. When he showed up at the door bearing a beautiful bouquet of brilliant yellow daffodils, I welcomed him in with a big enthusiastic hug. I was very aware of Mark's presence, and I paid much more attention to him than my other guests. It was his first time to meet my family and friends. The whole evening went well.

My sisters and my parents all approved. And during the party, the husband of one of my best friends took me aside to say, "He's a neat man, Shireen. He'd be good for you!"

The next few days I reflected on the party and on Mark. I felt so comfortable with him. I felt as if I'd known Mark for ages. And yet I realized I didn't really know much about him at all. He drew me out; he was such an interested listener. Yet he didn't talk much about himself.

So I prayed that God would give me the wisdom and the

sensitivity to ask the questions that would draw Mark out. I so much wanted to be patient and proceed at Mark's speed.

Mark called me on February 1 to ask when I might have a free day to spend with him. We settled on the nineteenth. But he didn't give me a clue as to what he had in mind. I could only wait and see.

In the meantime, we talked two or three times on the phone. He told me about his exciting plans to go to Hong Kong in April to design showroom vignettes for one of his clients—a wholesale furniture company—that was opening its first retail store in the Far East. I shared concerns about my work: the continued threat of layoffs that would cost me my job, because I had the least seniority of the school's home ec staff; my frustration with a particularly difficult student who wasn't dealing with the reality of her blindness; and more.

We shared on a spiritual level as well. Mark told me about some of the things he'd been learning in his Bible study. And he said he'd been thinking and praying for God's guidance about moving to the East Bay and buying a house in Oakland. I talked about my ongoing struggle in learning to accept death. In my journal I listed eight people I'd cared about who'd died recently. I was having an emotional struggle with the "why?" question, and I'd been praying for God to help me better understand the issue from his perspective.

Mark was such a good listener. And he knew just what to say to encourage me.

My day with Mark in February proved to be an eye-opening experience. We stopped by a client's retail hat shop, which was being remodelled, to see one of Mark's design projects in progress. Mark took me along to another client's home to get the woman's reaction to paint and wallpaper samples Mark had to show her. Then we went to see a house he was thinking about buying; while there he brainstormed ideas for fixing it up.

I appreciated the chance to see Mark at work. I was impressed by his manner with people—the clients we met as well as the workmen putting his plans into being.

I'd always thought of myself as a potentially creative person. But I felt almost intimidated by Mark's creative genius. (Some of that genius was obvious that day, and I learned more and more the longer I knew him.) He knew so much about construction and about lighting. He designed furniture and lamps. He was obviously gifted in floral and fabric design. He designed and sewed (on his own industrial machine) accessories such as pillows and wall hangings for some of his clients. He knew and loved music, studied Oriental art and culture for fun, was currently rehearsing for a part in a church play, and, on top of all that, he loved to cook!

There was so much I could learn from him. But it made me wonder, *What can I offer him? Just a womanly perspective on life, my home ec background, and an interest in helping people with special needs. Would that be enough to keep his interest?*

I thought I sensed a growing emotional investment in our relationship on his part. I didn't think it was just something I conjured up in my imagination. We seemed so in tune. I felt a sensitive, intuitive, non-verbal communication between us that I'd never experienced with any other man. I thought he sensed it too. At least I hoped he did.

I didn't want to push our relationship. I wanted to be sure of Mark's feelings. Meanwhile, I was feeling more and more sure of my own.

Finally, one evening late in March, just over three months after we'd met, I felt the time had come to share with Mark about the deepest hurt in my past. We were sitting in an old-fashioned ice cream parlor eating sundaes when I decided to tell him about Andrew. I guess part of the reason I was willing to be so vulnerable was the hope that my sharing would help him to feel more free to talk about his own past. But mostly, I just wanted him to know, to understand everything about me.

"It's been eight years ago this month that I was engaged," I said. And I went on to tell him about Andrew, our breakup because of Andrew's homosexuality, and the years of emotional pain I'd gone through as a result.

Mark listened intently. When I finally finished, he smiled and said, "That's very interesting, Shireen. Because eight years ago I also was engaged to a girl I thought I wanted to marry. But I broke off that relationship to pursue the gay lifestyle . . ."

CHAPTER TWO

MARK DIDN'T ADD MANY DETAILS that night, except to tell Shireen he'd been a part of the gay lifestyle for about seven years. That over time he'd found it less and less satisfying. And he'd given it up about a year and a half earlier as he'd begun a time of pilgrimage and soul-searching that eventually led him to a very real, personal relationship with Jesus Christ.

I just listened. And when Mark seemed to finish, I let the conversation drift another direction. I figured he would tell me more when he was ready; I didn't want to press him.

Strange as it may seem, Mark's admission didn't shock me. In a way, it didn't even surprise me. Looking back, I think I'd had an inkling, an intuitive feeling since the beginning of our friendship. I hadn't let it bother me. And now that the truth was out, I felt surprisingly undisturbed by Mark's revelation. Despite the pain of my past experience with Andrew, Mark's confession there in that ice cream parlor did nothing to alter the feelings I had for him.

Mark said he had changed. And I believed him.

But Shireen had no idea how much Mark had changed. In fact, she knew very little about his past life. Additional details were to surface slowly in the months and years ahead.

Mark Perry had been in college and engaged to be married when he enrolled in a psychology course entitled "Homosexual Perspectives." What he learned in that course seemed to explain for him some of the feelings he'd experienced growing up; it opened up the possibility in his thinking that he had a homosexual orientation. In his own words, "something was tugging me in that direction."

The course seemed to give Mark permission to quit resisting his feelings. He broke up with his fiancée and began associating with the homosexual community on his campus. Before long he'd established a sexual relationship with another man—a relationship that lasted for three years.

After he was out of school, Mark moved to Portland to manage a store, and his relationship ended. In Mark's words again: "I became blatantly gay—I didn't try to hide it. When the doors opened for me to come to San Francisco, I moved and started over. I was introduced to the homosexual scene here and I plunged in. Soon I was as much involved in the San Francisco gay community as anyone.

"I managed a store for a while right on Castro Street. I pursued relationships with people from every aspect of the gay community. I got into the leather scene and the hard-core cruise bars where little is said, you just go in, find someone who looks interesting and go home with him.

"I couldn't even guess the number, but I had many, many different sexual partners. The farther I went, the farther I had to go. I smoked dope, used cocaine occasionally, dropped acid—the whole trip.

"But no matter what I did, or how far I went in search of satisfaction, I began to realize my deepest needs weren't being met. I told myself, 'There has to be more to life than this quest for one more orgasm.' I felt trapped in a downward spiral I couldn't break out of."

At that point, Mark began his own spiritual journey. He explored mysticism, Eastern religions and read about various religious faiths. But he found nothing in any of his research that answered his questions or seemed to fit what he knew from experience to be true. Then his younger brother Bruce came to him and told him he'd just become a Christian; Mark listened with curious interest to Bruce's enthusiastic account of what had happened to him.

Finally, Mark said: "One night at home my eyes fell on an old black leather Bible my mother had given me. It'd been in my collection of books for years, though I'd never really noticed it before. I picked it up and started to read. I don't remember what passage I read, or even what it was about, but I remember it dealt very specifically with something I was experiencing that very day. And I thought, 'This is spooky. There's something to this.' It seemed almost like magic.

"So I promised myself I would begin reading the Bible and keep reading it until I got something out of it."

And he did. In the following days and weeks, Mark discovered what he read in the Bible often spoke clearly about issues hc was wrestling with daily in his life and his work. Things like values and priorities in life. It said much that rang true about love, commitment, integrity and service to others. The more he read, the more he wanted to read. And the more he wanted to believe what the Bible said.

When he read what the Bible said about homosexuality, Mark decided to change his behavior. He ended the relationship he was in and moved into another apartment by himself. He became celibate and pulled back from his associations and friends in the gay community.

Mark explained it this way: "I went through a cleansing process of burning my dope, my pornography and other things. As I got rid of each of these remnants of my past life, I felt a wonderful release inside. I knew I was doing the right thing."

Six months of gradual change went by before his older brother, John, who lived down in Fresno, invited Mark for a Christmas visit. Mark noted, "John and his wife, Kathy, are active Christians, and there was a special atmosphere in their home I couldn't quite put my finger on."

Mark told them about the changes going on in his life, and asked questions about some of the things he was reading in the Bible. The three of them began talking about Jesus and how the Bible says a person who asked Christ for forgiveness could begin a new life and have Jesus help him live it. And that's just what Mark did that Christmas Day.

Right away, John called and asked some friends to recommend a good church Mark could attend in San Francisco. So it was that Mark walked into the First Covenant Church of San Francisco that next Sunday. He didn't know a soul there. He had no idea how he'd be accepted. But he said, "I immediately felt right at home. I had prayed that God would bring others I could relate to, and within a couple weeks, I met an artist who had come out of homosexuality."

What followed was an exciting period of growth and learning for Mark—professionally and personally. Having worked for one of the top international designers in his field after he moved to San Francisco, Mark had gained enough confidence in his own talents to launch his own interior-design business. As Mark's reputation grew, so did his client list. But he struggled to reconcile his growing professional success with his newfound faith.

He read in the Bible where Jesus instructed his disciples to leave everything and follow him; so Mark began giving away all his possessions to his friends and planning to travel to Japan with the vague notion of being some kind of missionary. Not long after his well-meaning but indefinite plans for Japan fell through, Mark became enamored with some Christians' writings and teaching that promised God would honor those who prayed and lived with enough faith by granting them earthly, material success as well as spiritual and eternal rewards. He'd swung from one extreme to the other—from a "sacrifice everything" mindset to a "God wants me to have it all" belief.

His old friends thought Mark had gone off the deep end as some sort of fanatic Christian. But everyone knew he'd changed.

Mark had made a definite break from the gay lifestyle. It wasn't easy. He experienced deep feelings of loneliness and loss. Sometimes the temptation to turn back to the old patterns, the old lifestyle, grew strong. Mark spent many hours (alone or with one of his closest Christian friends) praying for strength to hold to the new course he felt was right.

Finally, gradually, he reached the point where he said, "Even thinking about my past behavior repulsed me." So determined was he to signify and solidify his change that he purposely studied and imitated the mannerisms of the straight men he now encountered at church and elsewhere.

Yet he hadn't embraced heterosexuality. He wasn't looking or even thinking about looking for any romantic relationship. He explained, "I was happy being a eunuch, if that's what God wanted."

Then he met Shireen.

After our ice-cream parlor conversation, Mark and I continued to talk on the phone from time to time. I thought now that he'd told me the little bit he had about his past, my continued acceptance and interest would encourage him to develop a closer relationship. But the conversations remained on the same friendly-but-never-romantic level. He'd give me a friendly peck of a kiss on the cheek when he'd see me, a polite European-style greeting he bestowed on various female acquaintances. Nothing more. So I began to wonder, with three months gone by, if Mark and I would ever be more than casual friends.

I didn't just sit around and wait for Mark to make all the moves, however. I woke up early one Sunday morning in March and decided to give Mark a call. "If you don't already have plans, how would you like to have company? I don't have anything going on today, and I haven't seen you for a while. I thought it would be nice to spend the day together." I couldn't believe I was doing this; it wasn't at all like me to be so aggressive.

"Sure, I'd like company," Mark agreed quickly. "In fact, I'm going to be baptized this afternoon and I'd be glad for you to be there."

I hurriedly dressed, got in my car and headed over the Bay Bridge into the fog-shrouded city of San Francisco. It was a very special day for me. I went with Mark to his church for the first time. We fixed a lunch at his apartment and then we went to the church where Mark and ten or twelve other people were baptized. There I had a chance to meet several of Mark's old friends from his former lifestyle; he'd invited them as a testimony of how he'd changed.

By the time we returned to Mark's apartment, he complained of feeling nauseated. I fixed him some chamomile tea for his stomach. But when I left to drive home a few minutes later, he was still resting uncomfortably on his daybed in his hillside apartment, looking out the front window over downtown San Francisco. I thought of him the whole drive home.

Tuesday morning I got a phone call. "Hi, Shireen. This is Mark."

"Are you okay?" I asked. "You sound terrible."

"I'm in the hospital."

"The hospital? What's wrong?"

Mark told me he'd gotten sicker after I left him Sunday evening. So he'd driven himself to the hospital Monday morning and had an emergency appendectomy a few hours later. He said he was fine, just tired and sore.

Mark's call had come just as I was about to leave for a graduate class in the city. So I promised to drop by the hospital and see him after my class.

On my way to school, I stopped at the San Francisco flower market, a giant wholesale center where florists from around northern California come to buy fresh flowers in the early morning hours. Since I'd done floral arrangements for a few weddings, I had a retailer's pass. I walked quickly through a warehouse door into a vast sea of fragrant colors. I stopped at only a couple booths, selected an assortment of spring flowers—tulips, astrum, daffodils and iris. I also selected an imported Italian vase I thought Mark would like, jumped back in my car and headed for campus. After dropping the flowers off in a friend's dorm room, I raced for my class.

Afterwards I returned to the dorm room for my flowers, which I arranged and rearranged in the vase a dozen times. Knowing Mark was an expert with flowers, I wanted the arrangement just right.

He said it was. And we had a nice visit before I headed across the bay again to my afternoon swing shift at the Orientation Center for the Blind. Almost every day that week I stopped after class and visited Mark.

One of those days it was raining. And my mobility-class teacher had us out on the streets in the Sunset district of San Francisco. (This mobility class was to train instructors who in turn teach blind people how to get around safely using their white canes.) The main thing I learned that morning was it's impossible to walk blindfolded around a city in the rain and have any idea where the puddles were or what gutters would be full of water. By the end of class my shoes and feet were so sopping wet that I stopped at a department store and bought a pair of dry socks and their cheapest pair of shoes so I could stop and see Mark without worrying about catching pneumonia.

The hospital released him that weekend. And Mark invited me to his apartment for dinner the first night he was home. We ate a delicious dinner, and I had an enjoyable time getting acquainted with Mark's mother, who'd come to take care of him for a few days. After the meal, his mom insisted on cleaning up and left the two of us pretty much to ourselves. We sat close together on his daybed couch as he paged through his favorite floral design book with me. Far below us spread the panoramic beauty of the city at night—the lights like a million jewels scattered against a black velvet drape.

Everything always seemed so special when I was with Mark. And so comfortable.

After that week of seeing each other almost every day at the hospital, we did talk more often on the phone. And we'd get together every week. We had reached a turning point in our relationship.

One evening after eating dinner at a friend's house, Mark

brought me home and we talked a while, sitting in my parents' living room. When the time finally came for Mark to leave, I walked him to the door. He turned to say goodbye and then drew me into an embrace with a warm, gentle kiss on the lips. I felt instant electricity again. That one short kiss meant so much that I was in the clouds for days.

Yet Mark still didn't make any verbal declaration of his romantic feelings for me. And I couldn't help wondering why. I was crazy about the guy. He had to know that. I felt certain there seemed to be a growing attraction for him, too, though he said nothing to encourage my feelings.

I found my own encouragement, however. One day, thumbing through my journal, I noticed an entry from back in November. In it I listed the qualities I'd thought necessary in any man I'd consider marrying: "Loves the Lord, gentle, interested in arts and culture, enjoys people, has a sense of humor, attractive to me, willing to be a team, business sense, likes to travel, accepting of people, enjoys working with his hands."

I hadn't thought about that list since the day I'd written it. But it described Mark Perry to a T. *All that and handsome too.*

Flipping a couple of pages later in the journal, I found another entry that had completely slipped my mind. I read, "Lord, please bring someone along who is just right for me." I'd written that prayer at the start of the very week I'd met Mark.

Suddenly, my doubts seemed to evaporate. I felt certain Mark Perry was the man God intended for me to marry. And I prayed God would soon get that same message through to Mark.

In April Mark took his long-anticipated Hong Kong trip. He left me the key to his apartment so I could water his plants, check his phone messages and collect his mail.

A week passed. Ten days. No word. I'd sent along a packet of little notes to be opened one on each day of his trip—to remind him of me. But I hadn't received so much as a postcard. And I missed him terribly.

One night a girlfriend and I decided to spend the evening in San Francisco and stay overnight at Mark's apartment. My mom called me there to tell me I'd received a letter from Mark in the mail that afternoon. I was so excited I asked my mother to open it right then and read it to me over the phone.

"Are you sure?" she asked.

"I'm sure! Open it!"

The letter told some of the things he was doing. Some of the things he'd seen. And he said he missed me! I would have liked him to say more. But I would settle for that. He missed me! There was hope.

While Mark remained hesitant to articulate his feelings for Shireen, those feelings were deepening nonetheless. A sampling of his own journal entries during his Hong Kong trip reveals his emotional state of mind.

On April 25, he described in some detail the elegance of his hotel and the restaurant where he ate dinner. And he wrote of his "sadness not being able to share this with a loved one." Because "my romantic nature is kindled."

The next day's entry described a Chinese wedding basket he'd purchased and said, "I do love being here. How I wish to share this experience with my wife-to-be."

Two days later he wrote, "I feel I've known Shireen all my life." And a one sentence prayer, "Let our love grow according to your will, Lord."

There was more to be done in Hong Kong than Mark planned. He'd shipped wallpaper and carpet from the States to be used in the various vignettes—mostly bedroom and dining-room settings—to be constructed for the displays. But he arrived to find the newly leased store practically bare. Walls for many of the vignettes hadn't even been built. So Mark directed Chinese construction crews in the execution of his designs, revamping some of his plans when he learned brick wasn't available. Only after the construction neared completion could he begin the more exciting, creative task of scouring Hong Kong's stores and shops for accessories that would compliment his client's furniture and give each of the vignettes an appealing, realistic feel.

Mark's scheduled two-week stay in Hong Kong stretched to three. But he still managed a brief stopover in Hawaii on the way home. And there, resting on the beach, he pondered and recorded in his journal some of his goals for the future.

His business goals centered on plans for courting and winning more international clients.

Among his personal goals he wrote: "Need to call about wedding plans. Go and visualize church. Must sit and have heart-to-heart talk with Shireen."

I met Mark's return flight at the airport, where he greeted me with an enthusiastic embrace and a big kiss. We went out to dinner, and I spent the entire meal thinking how wonderful it was to have him home. He seemed genuinely happy to be with me again. He laughed easily and excitedly told me about his Hong Kong adventure. And yet I sensed an underlying seriousness in his mood.

As I drove him back to his apartment, he told me he'd been struggling a lot with old feelings of guilt. About what, he didn't say. I didn't ask, because it didn't matter. Instead, I just listened to him express his feelings. And as we sat in my car, parked in his driveway, I reminded him of the promise of God's forgiveness in Psalm 103, verse 12, which says, "As far as the east is from the west, so far has he removed our transgressions from us."

He seemed to brighten just hearing that verse. And it felt so wonderful to be an encouragement to him for once. His optimistic, encouraging spirit had uplifted me so many times in the months I'd known him. It felt good to be on the giving end for a change.

As we continued to talk, Mark suddenly fell silent. For a few moments he looked at me in a strange way, with a look I'd never seen from him before. And after a few moments he said, "There's an aura of beauty around you tonight, Shireen."

> Mark described that moment from his perspective in a journal entry the next day. "I saw Shireen in a new light for the first time. Her beauty transformed her as we sat talking in the car. Her softness and fragileness became more evident, and the expression on her face changed from tension to I believe what was her natural state of innocence. I will never forget this transformation. Thank you, Lord, for this vision of Shireen."
>
> Later Mark was to describe what he saw as an "angelic aura" around Shireen. He felt it marked a new beginning in their relationship and in the way he thought about Shireen. And yet he articulated none of this at the time.
>
> And despite what he'd written in Hong Kong, despite his goal to "have a heart-to-heart talk with Shireen," something held Mark back. He still couldn't seem to voice his deepest feelings and desires.

I did sense a new level of commitment from Mark after his return from Hong Kong. But it was just a sense. And I didn't know whether or not to trust it.

Finally, one day I worked up the courage to assure Mark of my feelings and make myself vulnerable in hopes that he'd open up with me. I took a deep breath and just blurted it out: "I want you to know that I feel you're a very special gift from the Lord to me.

And I care a lot about you."

"Ditto," came his reply.

Just *ditto?* I couldn't believe my ears.

Ditto? How incredibly unromantic.

But heartening. For someone as much in love as I was, it didn't take much.

CHAPTER THREE

I WAS FURTHER ENCOURAGED ABOUT the progress of our relationship that spring when we made a weekend trip to the Fresno area where we stayed with Mark's aunt and uncle. That weekend also gave me a chance to meet Mark's brother John and his family, and to visit his grandparents in Hanford. I was a little surprised and a lot pleased when Mark's sister-in-law, Kathy, told me how excited everyone was that Mark had brought his "girlfriend" to meet the family.

So that's how he thinks of me? It was great to know, even if he wasn't the one who told me.

Maybe we were making progress.

Just as I was glad to meet Mark's family, I wanted him to get to know the special people I work with. So it made me feel supported and affirmed when he enthusiastically accepted my invitation to escort me to the retirement dinner for one of my colleagues. The dinner itself was a memorable night in our developing relationship. I was at first a little uncertain as to why he insisted on sitting across the table from me instead of beside me. But we'd no sooner gotten seated than he began playing footsie with me under the table. When I realized what he was doing and he realized I realized it, he got this sweet, sheepish grin on his face and a mischievous twinkle in his eye.

We were definitely making progress.

A few weeks after the weekend with his family, Mark and I joined my parents and my siblings for a long weekend at a cabin up in Mendocino County. My mother was touched that Mark had brought her a bouquet of flowers. During our stay there, my brother-in-law Barry made up a song about "Mark the Spark" and sang it for everyone several times in the course of the weekend.

I turned bright red and could have shot him the first time he started singing. But Mark laughed and didn't seem to mind. So I relaxed and enjoyed the silliness with everyone else. It was great having Mark fit in so naturally with my family.

One evening while we were there on the coast with my family, Mark and I took a long, arm-in-arm walk alone along the cliffs above the beach. We stood for a time listening to the pounding of the ocean down below. And we kissed as the moonlight reflected in long jagged lines of foam as breakers crashed up and down the shoreline.

The time and place seemed as good as any to voice the question on my mind. "Mark, where do you see our relationship going?"

Mark was silent. The sea pounded. And then he said, "I'm waiting on the Lord about our relationship. I know some wonderful things are in store for us. But I'm waiting on God's timing."

Okay. That answer sounded reassuring, even romantic, standing alone on a moonlit beach. It made me feel good.

But later, in the full light of the next morning, I realized I wasn't sure what his answer had meant. It made me wonder if he was thinking about marriage. Yet I wasn't any more certain of where I stood with Mark than before I'd asked.

The time Shireen and Mark spent with each others' families did, however, give them the time and the opportunity to learn more about their respective backgrounds.

Mark had been born in 1953 in Hanford, California, but his parents divorced when he was still a preschooler, and his mom moved the family a number of times back and forth between Oregon and California.

As Mark said, "My father didn't play a very big part in my life during my growing-up years." Yet, while he expressed good feelings for his current step-dad, Mark had felt the need in more recent years to re-establish regular communication and some sort of relationship with his biological father, who ran a general store and owned a ranch.

John, Mark's older brother, left home at age fifteen to go live with his dad, and in the process had maintained stronger ties with Mark's father's side of the family in central California. Mark, along with his younger brother Bruce and his half-sister Barbara, had lived with their mom and spent about half of their growing-up time in Oregon, where Mark eventually went to college and started out in business.

Mark still had a photo of his first room design, created at the age of twelve when he transformed his own bedroom to red and white decor with the help of some castaway curtains and bedspread and a bit of leftover paint. In analyzing this memory for Shireen, he said he thought he'd been motivated by a strong desire to create a space of his own where he could feel in control and find a little security in a world characterized by change and impermanence.

I had been born to Jack and Bev Irvine in 1954, in Afghanistan, where my father taught English as a second language, first for the Afghan government and then in a program jointly sponsored by the United States Agency for International Development and Columbia University. My folks eventually added three more children—Ronah, Marguerite and Jay—to the family. We lived for a time in Iran, Iraq and then Sacramento before finally settling in the East Bay when I was fifteen.

During high school, I volunteered as a reader for blind students. That experience sparked my special interest in visually impaired people. After high school, I spent a year studying in England before returning to California and enrolling in a junior college, and then transferring to San Francisco State University for my undergraduate degree.

Early during my college days, while working for a friend with multiple sclerosis, I met and talked with her occupational therapist who suggested the possibility of combining my home economics interest with rehabilitation. A senior-year field experience/practicum assignment at the Orientation Center for the Blind (OCB) confirmed in my mind that I could indeed make a meaningful difference in the lives of newly blind adults by teaching them adaptive daily living skills that would better enable them to cope with their disability.

Shireen continued to live with her folks in Oakland after she graduated from college and accepted a position at OCB. Her parents' roomy, English Tudor home was convenient to her work and a cheap alternative to the high California housing costs. But most of all, Shireen didn't know anyone she'd rather live with. The Irvines were a close, spiritually supportive family. Her parents were there for her when she wanted company or needed encouragement. But they also gave her room to be her own person and live her own life.

Mark and Shireen had come from very different family backgrounds. So while part of Mark appreciated the supportive closeness Shireen had with her family, another part of him felt the bond seemed a little too tight.

The better we got to know each other, the more I realized there was to learn about Mark. I'd never met anyone like him. Mark had a passion for life. He was so intense, so deliberate. So when he determined to change something—personally or professionally—he changed it, sometimes swinging from one extreme to the other. His shift from the "sacrifice everything" idea to the "God wants to give me health and wealth" viewpoint was a good example. Another was his change in dress: he'd gone from wearing casual, 501 Levis and colorful shirts to being a careful follower of the conservative, "dress for success" style.

Also, where he'd been something of a snippy, critical person in the past, he now worked hard (and effectively) to be a considerate person who deliberately and regularly affirmed others. He'd somehow gotten connected with Amway and had bought into the value of setting goals and positive thinking. He tended to be a real extremist in his positive thinking. But I found his determination and his complexity all the more interesting and admirable.

As time passed, there seemed to be more and more positive clues about Mark's attitude toward our relationship. Early that summer we were sitting outdoors on the deck of my sister's house, just the two of us, when Mark suggested we each get out our calendars and set aside days and times we could get together for the next three months. What that said to me, even if he didn't put it into words, was: "I'm serious enough about you to make sure we fit into each other's lives." It was a strong assurance for me that Mark wanted our relationship to continue and grow.

But the next few months were a confusing time of mixed messages from Mark. The more time we spent together, the more positive feelings I had and the more positive signs I saw that my relationship with Mark was growing toward marriage. Then something would happen—Mark would say or do something that would bring the doubts rushing back.

Once we were browsing together at an antique shop in a weathered old barn when Mark paused to look at some china on display. The set was incomplete—maybe seven dinner plates, eleven salad plates and an odd number of cups and saucers. "Do you like this china?" Mark asked.

It seemed a rather classic pattern—off-white with a simple gold trim on the outside edge. "Yes," I responded in what I thought was a non-committal tone. But I thought, *Why is he asking me?*

As he continued to examine the tableware, I wondered, *What does this mean? Is there some significance in our looking at china together?* He decided to buy the china, but then he didn't say anything more.

And a few weeks later, when Mark decided to move out of his apartment on Corbett to a smaller place, a studio apartment on Washington Street in the Pacific Heights district of San Francisco, I felt even more confused. He told me about his decision, but he didn't really discuss it with me. I helped him clean out his old apartment, but when I walked into his cramped new quarters I thought, *He's obviously not planning to make room in his life for me anytime soon.* And I felt very discouraged.

By the end of that summer I began regularly attending First Covenant Church of San Francisco with Mark every Sunday morning. Mark seemed comfortable with the fact that our lives were becoming more and more intertwined. And yet, that was about the time Mark admitted to me that he was wrestling with the question of whether or not God wanted him to remain single all his life.

Shireen's decision to begin going to church with Mark every week coincided with the arrival of a new pastor at First Covenant Church. Mike Ryan was a burly bear of a man, an ex-pro football player with a compassionate and enthusiastic spirit. Mark liked Mike right from the start, and Shireen hoped that a combination of Mike's spiritual leadership and friendship would encourage Mark's spiritual growth and provide him with a strong positive role model.

The two men did hit it off well. Mike had grown up in San Francisco as the son of a firefighter; so he and Mark shared a deep love for the city, its people and its problems. Mark appreciated and respected the depth of Mike's preaching and teaching. He regularly sought Mike's counsel.

I felt especially good about the fact that Mike very quickly began to appreciate Mark's spiritual sensitivity and his qualities of leadership; and Mike asked if Mark would be willing to lead a community Bible study. Mark and the leaders of several other Bible studies would meet with Pastor Mike every Sunday to study and discuss the passage to be covered in their group later in the week.

Mark took the challenge and thrived in the role of student and teacher. His Bible study, which began with two people, grew to twenty-five—it literally packed out his studio apartment. Some who came were church members, but others were just friends and acquaintances Mark invited—neighbors, and even a number of old friends from his days in the gay community. Shireen, who'd had some experience leading Bible studies during her college days, encouraged him in this leadership role by being a part of the study and by suggesting additional resources for him.

Mark put his positive, affirming people skills into practice, regularly writing "pick-me-up" notes and making encouraging phone calls to each member of his group to express his interest and concern. And his efforts paid off. Mike Ryan said, "I think more people came to our church and to Christ through Mark Perry's Bible study than through all the other twenty groups combined during my time at First Covenant. He was such a warm, engaging, enthusiastic person. People were just drawn to Mark.

"He was so obviously a talented man. Bright, spiritually sensitive, committed to excellence—in his work and every other area of life. Mark was a perfectionist—always demanding the best, most of all from himself."

Indeed, the last part of Mike Ryan's assessment was confirmed by an entry in Mark's own journal about this time which said: ". . . being productive and striving to succeed isn't bad. . . . I keep feeling I'm being dragged down to mediocrity every time I get ahead. I know I need to get my focus off myself and onto others and encourage them."

Not many people at First Covenant knew the story of Mark's past, but he told his pastor. Seeing the growing relationship with Shireen, Mike asked Mark directly about his current sexual feelings. "He assured me," Mike said, "that he had all the right urges. And that he was quite certain he'd have no trouble with heterosexuality when and if the time came to get married. I believed him. We had a very open and honest relationship."

Whatever uncertainties I had about the direction our relationship was going, Mark was wonderfully supportive of me during those months. He listened as I vented my emotions about the stresses

at work where a number of staff people still lived with the demor-
alizing threat of layoffs. He prayed with me and for me and
encouraged me as I wondered what I should do if I did lose my
job.

When my fifteen-year-old cousin Lara was diagnosed that fall
with acute promylectic leukemia, Mark would go with me to visit
her in the hospital and even went to the family conference where
the doctor spelled out the disheartening prognosis that the rare,
fast-acting cancer gave Lara only a short time to live. The day
Lara died, a few weeks later, I waited at home and tried to reach
Mark every few minutes by phone. I wanted to let him know
about Lara, but he wasn't at his apartment and I didn't know
where he was or when he'd be back. I found out later he'd just
left a meeting at church when he felt led to drive to the hospital
to see Lara. He'd gotten there shortly after she died and had
stayed to be a support for Lara's family.

While on the one hand he could be so supportive and spiritually sensitive, Mark could also be quite demanding. Though I
appreciated and respected him for his honesty, I sometimes
wished he weren't so confrontational. He took me to task a
number of times about needing to say what I thought and not
hold back on my feelings. I like to ponder things before I react;
but Mark continually challenged me to take risks and be more
spontaneous.

One beautiful, sunshiny day we packed a picnic lunch and
drove north across Golden Gate Bridge, through Mill Valley and
up the long winding road to the top of Mount Tamalpais. There
on the windswept heights, we spread out a blanket, unpacked our
food and ate our picnic, sprawled on the soft carpet of grass. The
blue Pacific stretched to the western horizon on our right. Below
and in front of us lay the Golden Gate, San Francisco's skyline,

and the entire bay in spectacular panorama.

As we ate and soaked in the awesome beauty, Mark told me this spot was a special place for him. He called it "one of the seven jewels of San Francisco" because of the outcroppings of jade-like rock. I asked what the other six jewels were, and he said he'd like to show me someday.

We had a glorious afternoon in the outdoors. We talked, laughed and reveled in the beauty before us and in each other's company. I couldn't have been happier. But before we left, Mark gave me another one of his self-improvement lectures about the value of positive thinking and the need to quit focusing on my negative feelings and frustrations—those things that were discouraging me—particularly regarding my work. I was noticeably quieter coming down the mountain than I had been going up.

That night I asked myself: "Does Mark want me to be perfect before he'll marry me? Sometimes he seems to push character change faster than I'm able to handle it."

A couple weeks later I wrote: "I'm having difficulty with some of Mark's responses toward me lately as he is working through whether he should ever be married or not. Lord, help me to accept what you want. You know I really desire to be married—to Mark. He seems so perfect for me. If he isn't, please change my heart. I don't want the hurt and pain again of a breakup. But now is better than later. Maybe I've been pushing too much."

Yet I'd tried to be patient. And I'd prayed continually that if Mark wasn't the man for me that God would clearly show me. It seemed every time I'd prayed that, something positive would develop in our relationship and I'd once again get such a strong feeling of peace about Mark.

But I also got an unsettled feeling whenever anyone asked me about our relationship. I never knew how to respond or what to say. And my awkwardness spawned new doubt. Mark was with me at my sister Marguerite's wedding and was witness to a few of the well-meaning relatives and friends who smiled, patted me on the arm, and wondered aloud, "When is it going to be Shireen's turn?" I was halfway tempted to point to Mark and say, "Ask him!" But instead I'd just smile gamely and say something innocuous like, "Oh, I don't know" or "I'll certainly let you know."

It wasn't as if Mark showed no signs of a growing commitment. Early in the fall he'd said he thought it time we each wrote down our personal goals and plan to talk about them together. I'd made a list of mine, including: "Want to be married by the first of the year." But then a couple months went by, and Mark never made time to talk about our goals.

We actually reached the point where we'd talk about the subject of marriage—but in general terms. Mark said he didn't think he could consider marriage until he got his business more securely established. While his design work did seem irregular—either feast or famine—I didn't need to feel we'd be financially secure before I'd commit myself to marriage.

I was ready. And I began to hope something more would develop in December.

At Christmas the two of us drove down to Fresno, where we celebrated his family Christmas with John and Kathy and their three girls on Christmas Eve. We were all opening presents around the tree Christmas Eve, when Mark presented me with a small gift-wrapped box. I sensed excitement in him as he waited for me to cautiously unwrap it. And I began to wonder if, just maybe, he was going to surprise me with a ring right here in front of everyone.

Inside the box was an Oriental, yellow-cloth jewelry envelope. *Could it really be?* I unzipped and opened the pouch to find . . .

a set of beautiful pearl earrings. "Oh, Mark! They're gorgeous!" They were. And I loved them. But deep in my heart I couldn't help feeling a twinge of disappointment.

"I bought them for you in Hong Kong," Mark said.

Hong Kong? That's more than eight months ago, I thought. *He was serious enough to buy me pearl earrings eight months ago, and he's waited till Christmas to give them to me?* Mark Perry was a very patient man. Painfully patient.

The next morning we left Fresno before five to drive back up to Oakland for Christmas with my family. That afternoon, Mark decided, since Christmas is Mike Ryan's birthday, we should bake Mike's favorite cake that his mom always fixed him when he was a kid—angel food lathered with whipped cream and bananas. So we did and then surprised him by delivering it that evening.

We couldn't stay long at Mike and Donna's that night, but we set plans to get together with them for breakfast on Monday, January 2. Not many restaurants were open that morning before all the big college bowl games, but we finally found a place on Lombard Street. Neither Mark nor I had yet gotten the chance to know Donna very well, so much of our time that morning was spent getting acquainted. But sometime toward the end of breakfast, Mike asked where we were in our relationship.

I'd talked around the issue too many times when people had asked. So I simply told Mike and Donna the truth. I said I loved Mark and was convinced he was the man God intended for me and "I'm ready to make a commitment to marriage."

Mike looked to Mark and asked pointblank, "Then what's keeping you from getting married, Mark?"

"Well, uh, . . . " Mark couldn't give much of a reason.

The subject was dropped. But I hoped Mike's blunt question would be what it took to get Mark moving.

After breakfast with Mike and Donna, we headed back to Mark's place to prepare dinner for a couple Mark had invited over that evening. On the way, Mark realized he had a problem: "How can I serve dinner at my apartment? I don't even have four chairs for my table." Yet almost as soon as he anticipated the complication, he had a solution. We drove to a little secondhand furniture store Mark knew about—amazingly, it was open. Mark found a set of six classic Bentwood Prague chairs and paid thirty-five dollars for them. We took them back to his apartment, re-covered the seats with some off-white silk fabric Mark had left over from some previous project, touched up the knicks and scratches with a black Magic Marker, and had four elegant-looking chairs around his table in time for dinner. And I was reminded again how much I loved Mark for his creative, we'll-do-what-it-takes, spontaneous spirit.

Yet the waiting couldn't go on forever. And Mike's bluntness with Mark prompted me to press the issue.

My graduate class was going to New York for a couple of weeks in early January to visit organizations working with the blind. On the day we were to leave, before I said good-by to Mark, I laid my feelings on the line. "In some ways I feel like we're already married. Yet we're not. Our relationship can't go on like this forever. Some decision needs to be made." It wasn't exactly an ultimatum, but telling him like I did just before I left town, the implication was clear—we needed to resolve this issue when I got back.

Everywhere I went in New York, every interesting building I noticed, every museum I visited, I thought, "Mark would like this. I wish he were here." And I wondered what he was deciding about me, about us. When I talked to him on the phone from New York, he didn't give me a clue.

Part of the reason may have been that Mark was extremely busy while she was gone with Market Week for his wholesaler clients—the time of year when clients wanted their showroom displays redesigned to feature their new product lines. So Mark put in many extra-long days.

But part of the problem had to be Mark's inner struggle with the decision he knew had to be faced. Mark had read a number of Christian books Mike Ryan recommended on sexuality and marriage. And he'd assured Mike he had no doubts about a positive healthy sexual relationship in marriage. Yet he had to wonder about his past and how it would impact a marriage relationship with Shireen.

He recorded some of his more general feelings of uncertainty in his journal: "I now have a lot of creative time for myself. Would I have this time in the future? Shireen is used to a lot of activity around her all the time. Will she be happy with just me? Or alone?

". . . When I feel clung to, I have a tendency to pull back and push away, even though that's not what I really want. Is that natural? What do I do?"

Yet to add to his confusion, he admitted to himself in writing, "No one is more in love than I am."

Still, when Shireen returned from New York, nothing was said about the "ultimatum."

Knowing Mark's appreciation for special dates and occasions, I told myself he probably had something special in mind for my thirtieth birthday. And he did. He gave me a beautiful cloisonné pen, a prize pen he'd bought for his pen collection when he'd been in Hong Kong. I knew how special the pen was to him, so I took the gift as positive sign. Yet my birthday had come and gone with no further mention of the real issue.

A couple days later, Mark called. "What about June?" he asked.

"What do you mean?" I responded.

"Think about it," he said.

Suddenly it hit me. "You mean to get married?"

"Yes."

"It sounds good to me!"

Finally! Mark is ready to get married! For such a creative, romantic guy, the proposal was decidedly unromantic. But it didn't matter at all. *YES!* I was going to marry Mark Perry!

That night Mark made this brief entry in his journal in very bold letters: "Shireen and I are officially engaged! Praise the Lord!"

CHAPTER FOUR

AS WE TALKED THAT WEEK, IT QUICK-
ly became apparent June would not be the best time for a
wedding. I wouldn't graduate from my master's program until
then. Meantime I had a full-time job plus a full-time school
load, and there would be no time or energy to enjoy planning
a wedding. So Mark and I made the mutual decision to set the
wedding date for September 1. Labor Day weekend would make
it easier for out-of-town relatives to come.

Mark called my parents to tell them he had something he
wanted to talk to them about. And that Saturday morning, he
arrived early at my folks' house for a special birthday breakfast
honoring my sister Marguerite. Ronah and Barry were already

there, so Mark and I took Mom and Dad into another room. And Mark began talking about his feelings for me, how our relationship seemed to be growing . . .

My dad, beaming from ear to ear, interrupted him. "Mark!" he declared, "We'd be thrilled to have you in our family."

"No," Mark said. "Please. Wait a minute, you have to let me finish my spiel!" So he said what he'd prepared to say as my parents and I sat grinning. When he finished, my dad laughingly redeclared his welcome of Mark into our family, and my parents embraced us both. When we went out to tell Ronah and Barry, there were more hugs all around. But we all agreed not to say a word about it when Marguerite and Ed arrived. It wasn't until we'd all gathered around the table and said grace, that I said, "Marguerite, there's something Mark and I wanted to tell you. We're engaged."

Marguerite screamed with joy and exclaimed: "That's the greatest birthday present!" She didn't seem to mind a bit that we'd upstaged her birthday celebration.

So much needed to be done those next few months. So much for the two of us to talk about. So many decisions to be made. I had to finish school. We needed to finalize wedding plans. And in discussing where we would live, we decided to look for a house to buy. And that meant a whole new set of decisions and discussions.

Agreeing that we wanted to start our lives together in the strongest possible manner, Mark and I decided to see a Christian counselor for premarital counseling. The plan was for the counselor to meet with us each individually and also as a couple. After the first few sessions, the counselor told me he saw indications of some deep communication problems in our relationship. He foresaw problems for me as a wife because he felt Mark held an idealistic view of his mother and had her up on a pedestal. And he called Mark a "song and dance man" who relies on vague statements to avoid sharing his deepest feelings and thoughts.

But none of what the counselor was telling me emotionally prepared me for his conclusion: "Shireen, I don't think you and Mark should get married."

I went home in tears.

I respected the counselor. I felt that his assessment of Mark was true, just as his judgments of my own shortcomings in communication were on target. Yet I just couldn't accept his final assessment. He didn't understand Mark like I did; I knew Mark wasn't afraid of change and that when he saw a weakness or a problem in himself, he would work on it. I'd seen and admired the deliberate, disciplined way Mark would tackle any job that needed doing. This would be no different. I felt certain of it. And after all the waiting, I felt more certain than ever that Mark was the one God wanted me to marry.

The end of May we went to the counselor together. We asked him, "How long would you give us to work on our communication problems? How long do you think it would take before you would feel certain whether or not we could overcome the difficulties you see?"

He thought for a few moments. I could read the doubt on his face as he rubbed his chin and sighed. "I don't know," he said. "Maybe ninety days."

"Okay," I said. "It's just over ninety days till the wedding. We have the time. If we can't make enough progress by then, we can cancel the wedding!" But I felt confident we wouldn't have to do anything that drastic. I knew I was willing to make whatever changes were necessary and I felt Mark was too.

That's not to say the summer was easy. We each had regular sessions with our counselor, who continued to work with Mark about his relationship to his mother. He gave us both assignments to discuss and work through together. That, in addition to our continuing house search and the wedding plans, meant we had a lot to communicate about.

The communication problems proved complex. I tend to intellectualize and internalize my feelings without expressing them. I'd clam up when Mark was angry or when I got upset about something. And when I shared thoughts and opinions, I did so without clearly communicating the emotions behind them to Mark. As a result, because I had such a hard time putting emotion to my words, Mark had a difficult time understanding or reading my feelings.

Mark, on the other hand, had the opposite problem of not being able to articulate the thoughts behind his feelings. We went round and round this subject when I'd try to get him to explain the rationale behind a creative idea or feeling he had. He argued that there was simply a difference between the intellect and intuition. That he couldn't put into words what he knew and felt intuitively. And when I pressed him to try, he read that as a lack of trust in him.

So we talked and talked and worked on our communication all summer. And we planned our wedding together.

Since I'd been a wedding consultant on numerous weddings, I had definite ideas about what I wanted. But I also wanted the benefit of Mark's creativity in the planning. He seemed reluctant to say much at first—perhaps he was trying to give me creative room—or perhaps it was that he felt I should make the decisions since I was the one paying the wedding costs out of my savings. But eventually, with continued encouragement, I got him involved in discussing the specifics.

We didn't agree on everything to begin with. He thought my desire not to have any attendants seemed radically nontraditional. I explained my reasons—that I wanted the focus of the day to be on our union before God, that I didn't want the distraction that attendants, flower girls and ring bearers often can be. Plus, I pointed out that the original, traditional purpose of attendants as the witnesses (and often only guests) at a wedding ceremony could be served just as well by the entire congregation attending our wedding. Even after hearing all my rationale—more than once—he only reluctantly acquiesced.

We did, however, agree on most of the details. And on our overall goal. We both very much wanted our wedding to be a memorable declaration of our love for each other and to be a powerful testimony as to the meaning of Christian commitment and marriage for everyone who would come.

The theme we settled on was "contemporary elegance." And I soon began to worry that our demanding artistic tastes exceeded our modest budget. But friends offered to do the flowers and the cake at cost. Bob Hartmann, a designer friend of Mark's, who uses and creates theatrical props for special events and corporate parties, agreed to handle the decor and lighting at the church as well as the decorations for our reception. And he made connections with a caterer he worked with for the best possible price on a buffet. As all the plans slowly fell into place, I realized we were going to have the first-class celebration we'd wanted for much less than what it might have cost.

On June 30, we signed the papers to buy a house—a small, two-bedroom Victorian row house on San Francisco's Potrero Hill. We'd be just a few blocks away from bayside shipyards, only ten or fifteen minutes from downtown and access to the

Bay Bridge—my daily route to work. Mark moved in at the end of July.

And near the end of August, Mark and I went together for our last scheduled counseling session before our wedding day. Our ninety days were up.

Our counselor sat in an overstuffed chair, looking across his office coffee table to where we sat on his couch. He smiled as he shook his head. "Well, you did it. I didn't think you could, but you two have made tremendous progress. I think there are some areas you still need to work on. But I don't see any reason why you shouldn't get married."

The wedding was on.

And what a wedding it was!

Bob Hartmann transformed the entire front of the First Covenant Church sanctuary into a wall of shimmering candlelight that reflected off the organ pipes, which were crowned from behind with a gentle hue of pink light. Pastor Mike Ryan slipped into the upstairs balcony to check out the setting during the preliminary music, recorded selections of synthesizer and flute which Mark and Shireen had selected to be played over the sound system from the balcony. "I felt intimidated," Mike admitted. "The music and the lighting were so spectacular."

Mark's and Shireen's brothers read a variety of Scriptures about love and commitment. All those in the congregation took part, first by singing "El Shaddai," a contemporary worship song made popular by Amy Grant, and by pledging their support and blessing to Mark and Shireen's union. Mike gave a short homily about the meaning of Christian marriage, and Mark and Shireen pledged themselves to one another with vows they had written.

I felt a little shaky at first, but as we sang "El Shaddai," Mark put his arm around me, and I felt a true sense of peace and calm.

Looking into my eyes, Mark vowed: "By the choice of God and by the choice of my heart, I take you, Shireen, to be my wife, that together we may be one. I promise you my deepest love, my unselfish devotion, and my tenderest care. Because Christ Jesus is the most important person in our lives, we will continue to seek his most perfect will, serving him and praising him together. I love you, Shireen. And therefore, throughout life, no matter what may lie ahead of us, I pledge you my life as a loving, faithful husband until the Lord returns or until death parts us."

Softly at first, I began my response to him: "Mark, God has prepared me for you. I receive you as my husband with much joy. I appreciate the many fine qualities you bring to our marriage. I will honor your goals and dreams. And daily seek wisdom in ministering to your emotional, spiritual, physical, intellectual and creative needs. I will affirm you, encourage you and edify you. I love you, Mark. Through all the changing experiences of life, whether sorrow or joy, darkness or sunlight, I choose to be to you all I am as a faithful, loving wife, companion, friend and lover. And this commitment I make for as long as we both shall live or until Jesus Christ returns."

A few minutes later, after we exchanged rings, Mike Ryan pronounced us husband and wife. And as Mark took me into his arms for the kiss, almost four hundred people burst into boisterous, spontaneous applause.

The reception turned out to be every bit as memorable as the wedding itself. For a surprisingly affordable price, Shireen and Mark rented the Green Room of the city's imposing, stone War Memorial Veteran's Building—a building which also housed the city's Museum of Modern Art and the Hearbst Theatre. The Green Room, a recital hall of classic design with a forty-foot ceiling and large masonry pillars, looked the epitome of "contemporary elegance." It offered a setting befitting a royal reception—with an open-air marble balcony offering a vista of San Francisco's Civic Center between its massive Greek-revival pillars.

Guests were a varied lot. Some of Shireen's colleagues from OCB came, as did a number of Mark's business associates. Members of the Irvine family met and mingled with the Perrys for the first time. New friends from church met old friends from Castro Street, college and childhood.

One of the reception's special features was traditional Afghan folk dancing for everyone who would join in the fun, with authentic Afghan music, courtesy of a group of Afghan immigrants, four of whom had lived with Shireen's family when they first came to America. After that, Mark and Shireen led off the ballroom dancing with a waltz.

Along with the bountiful buffet, the reception featured the traditional cake cutting and a toast made to the couple's happiness with glasses of sparkling cider. The joyous, festive mood struck Mike Ryan as "the most fun wedding I've ever been a part of" and "a truly special day." Marguerite pulled Shireen aside and whispered what many people were feeling: "Shireen, this is a dream wedding."

It was a wedding day far beyond my greatest expectations. I felt excited and comfortable. I felt the most feelings of happiness that I'd ever felt in my life, more happiness than I'd ever imagined. It did feel like a wonderful, romantic dream, and yet I was alert and relaxed enough to truly enjoy seeing and talking with friends and relatives, some of whom I'd not seen for years.

After the reception, Mark and I left to spend our first night together in our very own home. Mark carried me across the threshold. Then he put soft music on the stereo and lit votive candles he'd placed earlier in the window and on the small

Japanese tansu chest we would use as a nightstand. And then we went to bed and shared the full expression of our love as husband and wife.

There was no awareness of time. The warmth and romance of that Saturday night blended into Sunday. And it wasn't until Monday morning when we walked onto the plane that would carry us to our Hawaii honeymoon that we left our private world and re-entered reality.

The honeymoon couldn't have been more beautiful. The scenery was gorgeous. And Mark was a warm, gentle, wonderful lover. We were still in Hawaii when I finally made my first journal entry after the wedding. I wrote: "Coming to a deeper understanding of my own body has been marvelous. It boggles my mind to realize how man and woman are created to be together. Yet it's wonderful. Lord, you knew what you were doing!

"To think I'm married! Mrs. Mark Perry!" It was the culmination of all my dreams. The wellspring of incredible happiness.

But honeymoons can't last forever. Going back to work after two weeks of heaven seemed like an emotional letdown. And making the adjustment to living with another person who has different habits and his own ways of doing things proved a bigger challenge than I'd imagined.

As a designer, Mark had definite ideas for decorating the house. Sometimes I felt too intimidated by his genius to even voice my opinions on things I'd always imagined doing when I became a wife with a house of my own.

Everything had to be just so to suit Mark's designer eye. For example, he couldn't ever just stack our plates, dishes and glasses on the open shelves of our kitchen; he had to place them in an artistically pleasing arrangement. And while I could appreciate the results of his ideas when he got them implemented, I wanted to know what he was doing and why so I could help. I wanted to work as a team. But Mark still couldn't clearly articulate what he was doing as he did it; he preferred showing, not talking. So we continued to struggle to learn how to work effectively together on projects.

I so wanted to be the wife I'd vowed to be at our wedding—to minister to Mark's emotional, spiritual, physical, intellectual and creative needs. But I seemed to be having trouble in the creative area. Mark felt he wasn't getting enough outside stimulation to maintain his creativity. I felt as if I were failing him in that area.

Yet it wasn't as if our marriage was full of problems. For the most part it was great. And one of the early highlights came as a real surprise. At a church board meeting, Mark heard a presentation about the work of Charles Colson's Prison Fellowship and a specific upcoming program where five inmates were to be furloughed to take part in a community service project and a time of intense Bible study. He immediately thought of the Bible reference in Matthew 25:36, 40 where Jesus said, "I was in prison and you came to visit me. . . . I tell you the truth, whatever you did for one of the least of these brothers of mine, you did for me."

Mark felt we ought to volunteer to host one of the furloughed inmates for the two-week program. So when he came home from his meeting, he asked me to consider it. I wasn't too sure at first, but that Sunday at church, after seeing a promotional film that told about such Prison Fellowship programs, I turned to Mark and said, "Let's do it."

That's how we came to know a very impressive young man

named Loren, who became a real friend to both of us during his two-week stay in our home. A number of people expressed surprise that we opened our home like that: they exclaimed, "You've only been married a month!" But when we'd bought our house, we'd both agreed that we wanted it to be a place God could use. This just happened to be the first opportunity that came along. And it was such a positive experience that I felt very grateful for Mark's sensitivity and generous spirit that prompted him to propose the idea.

I found much to appreciate about Mark. He was so sweet and expressive of his love for me. On November 1, two months after the wedding, he gave me a funny card and wrote on it, "Happy Monthiversary #2. You're the best thing that ever happened to me. All my love, M."

He never missed a chance to celebrate a monthiversary. But he didn't wait for special occasions to be sensitive. One day at work, in the midst of an especially tough week, I found a piece of lined notebook paper in my purse; on it he'd written, "Honey, How blessed I am to be married to you. How I love you. Thank you for all your love. I'll be praying for you this week. Relax, pray and spend some quality time with the Lord." And he signed it with seven hugs and kisses.

We had an exciting fall together. Mark's business continued to grow. In September, he hired an office manager to handle the increasing multitude of details. In November he hired another designer to help him with the creative load required by a growing list of clients.

The addition of a payroll put a serious drain on the cash flow, especially when the number of projects suddenly dropped off in the usual pre-holiday slump. We were pretty much limited to my paycheck for several weeks there, which meant we had to make tough decisions about which bills to pay when. Yet to Mark, the hiring of two employees signalled a promising future; his business was definitely on the way up. And I shared his excitement.

One evening early in December, I fixed a special dinner of game hen, rice and vegetables, and we took our spontaneous picnic to the San Francisco Yacht Club Marina. We ate looking out over the bay, with Alcatraz out to the right and the sun setting beyond the Golden Gate Bridge to our left. We spent much of our time brainstorming the final details for the Christmas open house we planned for family and friends. And afterwards we went to one of Mark's favorite haunts, Cost Plus Importers, to look for creative ideas and pick up a few little items for our party.

> That evening Mark wrote in his journal, "Thank you, Lord, for my lovely wife, for her qualities that beautify her more each day. What a dinner–a surprise picnic on the marina road. With the orange lights of the Golden Gate Bridge appearing as Christmas lights spanning the bay. How I'm beginning to experience the pleasure of little things and the joy they bring."

The world was beautiful. And we'd never been happier.

Mark went in for a routine physical checkup in mid-December. His right big toe had nagged him for weeks with redness and swelling. The doctor prescribed an antibiotic for the infection and sent him home. His blood work and everything else seemed normal.

The morning of our open house Mark finally finished installing the spot lighting for our entry hall. And we both thoroughly enjoyed the forty or fifty friends and relatives who stopped in to see our home and share our holiday treats. We'd talked a lot about starting our own family holiday traditions, and we decided an annual open house would be one of them.

That night as we rehashed the successful day's ventures, Mark complained that he felt absolutely exhausted. "And," he said, "I don't really know why. I haven't done any more than usual today."

I didn't think much of his comment at the time. I simply chalked it up to the aftermath of an emotionally exciting and fulfilling day.

For my birthday in January, Mark gave me a card with an oriental-style painting of a hibiscus flower, perhaps because he sometimes called me his "precious flower." Inside the card said, "Like a rare flower, love must be treated gently. For it is priceless."

Mark's business picked up again after the first of the year. He got particularly excited about the chance to work on a two-thousand-square-foot addition to an exclusive house originally designed by a protégé of Frank Lloyd Wright. "It's just the kind of design project I've always wanted," he said. He believed the job could end up being featured in *Architectural Digest* and help boost his business to a new level. He was just as excited about the chance to work with the primary architect on the project—an extremely talented and creative professional who'd taught at Oxford and made a name for himself in his profession. I enjoyed seeing Mark so creatively stimulated by what he called a "dream" job.

But at the same time Mark began anticipating his professional future, he was growing more and more concerned about his health. The swelling in his toe bothered him much more than he let on to Shireen. And he'd noticed a small hard nodule, high on the back of his neck, and it seemed to be growing. A small purplish spot appeared first on his side. Then a couple of weeks later he noticed another on his arm.

One day at the end of February, Mark showed Shireen the spot on his arm and said he was going back to the doctor. He didn't tell her what he feared, what he didn't want to believe.

In the early to mid-80s, the current medical thinking on AIDS was that the disease had a three-year incubation period as an outside limit. Though he'd never said so to anyone, that was one of the reasons Mark had proceeded so slowly in his relationship with Shireen. When they were finally married, three years had passed since his last homosexual activity. Everything Mark had read told him he was safe. But he also knew the signs and he was worried.

The doctor who examined the spots on Mark's arm and side decided to do a biopsy. He told Mark he wanted to run a blood test for AIDS, using the HIV antibody test which had just become available. And he wanted him to come back the next day for an additional battery of nuclear medicine tests.

When I got home from work that Tuesday evening, Mark told me the doctor had done a biopsy on one of the spots and wanted him back at the hospital for more tests the next day. "He thinks I may have AIDS!"

AIDS? My mind must have gone numb with shock. I don't remember feeling or saying anything. Except numb disbelief. Neither of us said much. And though my mind was a jumbled maze of thoughts, there was one thing I knew with clarity: *I am going to love Mark through this crisis with God's unconditional love. Mark will need to know that he is loved.*

After supper Mark turned on the television and tried to tune out reality with some forgettable, made-for-TV movie. I lay down on our bed beside him in hopes that mindlessly watching the video images would short-circuit my still-racing thoughts.

Instead, the story—about a woman trying to choose whether or not to give up a relationship—triggered the terrible thought:

I don't want to lose Mark! And I may not even have a choice. At that thought, all the emotions broke through the dam. And I began to weep uncontrollably. Mark turned off the TV and held me in his arms.

"I don't want to lose you!" I sobbed, when I'd regained enough control to get out the words. "I couldn't live without you." Mark held me tight and kissed me and said he didn't want to lose me either. And we cried together.

And when we ran out of tears, we consoled each other by quietly, gently making love. Without a thought of needing any protection.

Wednesday Mark went in for the additional tests. He was to get the biopsy report on Thursday. By the time we awakened Thursday morning, I'd convinced myself that all our worries were for nothing. Mark was going to be fine.

Thursday, March 8, 1985, while Shireen was at work, Mark went in to get the hematologist's report on his biopsy results. The tests were positively conclusive, according to Mark's doctor. "Kaposi's sarcoma." The rare, incurable skin cancer common in those with AIDS.

When Mark asked the doctor for a prognosis, the man said he couldn't be sure. His best guess was, "You may have six months to live."

CHAPTER FIVE

MARK PERRY LEFT HIS CAR PARKED
at St. Mary's Hospital and set out walking along the streets of San
Francisco, trying to sort out his feelings and absorb the impact of his
doctor's words. It seemed his worst nightmare had come true. After
God had so dramatically changed his life, after all this time, after
marrying Shireen and beginning a new life together, after everything—he had AIDS.

Some time later he found himself walking into First Covenant
Church. He'd walked three miles from the hospital.

Pastor Mike Ryan recalled: "When I looked up from my desk to
see Mark through the glass of my office, I rose and opened the door
to invite him in. He sat down and I shut the door.

"Mark had told me the previous Sunday that he was expecting to get test results about a spot on his arm. He hadn't voiced any concern that it might be AIDS, but we both had our suspicions.

"Sitting in my office, he began to talk me through all that had happened. Starting with his toe, the lump on his neck, the spots on his skin and the doctor's decision to do a biopsy. He told me the diagnosis he'd gotten that morning—the spots were indeed Kaposi's sarcoma, one of the most certain symptoms of AIDS. 'And,' he concluded, 'the doctor says I have maybe six months to live.'

"He wept. And the two of us wept together. 'It's so unfair!' he declared. He talked about his love for Shireen, how they were just newlyweds and how he so much wanted to spend his life with her.

"When there was nothing else for either of us to say, we prayed. And I set a time for Mark and Shireen to meet together with Donna and me.

"I offered to drive him back for his car. But he said he wanted to walk. So I watched him go. Then I prayed, 'Lord, what a great way this could be to bring glory to yourself. Here's a guy who's been changed and brought out of the gay lifestyle. Now you can show yourself and your power by healing Mark from AIDS and letting the gay community truly see what you can do.' "

That afternoon Mike Ryan called a surgeon friend at Minnesota to ask, "What is this Kaposi's sarcoma?"

"Is it an AIDS diagnosis?" the doctor asked.

"Yes," Mike replied.

"Then he's a dead man," the doctor said.

I don't remember Mark's words, or even how he told me when I got home from work that afternoon. *Six months?* I remember thinking there had to be some absurd mistake. I knew virtually nothing about AIDS except that it was a terrible, incurable disease. And Mark was so healthy.

"We both have an appointment with Dr. Smoot on Monday," Mark said. "He wants to discuss AIDS with us and talk about what we ought to say to our friends and families."

Mark was so matter-of-fact. I guess we were both in shock.

But the turmoil in Mark's mind spilled out into his journal that night in a stream of half-thoughts. He wrote: "Mixed feelings of grief, sorrow, cheated out of life. Repercussions from past generations' mistakes. Tears, hurting. What to do with business, with Shireen. What about Shireen's safety? Thoughts about ought-tos and ought-not-tos. The fears of how to tell family and friends. Questions to God: Why me? How is God to be glorified in this? . . . All through this there is a peace of God. . . . What does this mean, my Lord? . . . How I thank God for Mike and Donna!"

Since Mike and Donna Ryan were the only people who knew, they invited us over for dinner the next evening to talk. After we ate, the four of us took a drive up to Twin Peaks, another spot Mark considered one of the gems of San Francisco. We pulled into a parking spot at the vista point and sat in the car to talk. A beautifully sparkling city spread out beneath us. And in the distance, the night lights of Oakland, Alameda and Berkeley rimmed the blackness of the bay. More than a million people lived within our sight, living out their own private dramas within the walls of their houses and apartments. Yet I may as well have been alone in the universe with my thoughts.

I still wasn't recognizing or allowing any feelings to surface, only thoughts, which raced through my mind in a chaotic stampede. At one point I thought Donna was crying. But the mood in the car was more sober than emotional.

We got out of the car after a while to walk and finally sit on the stone retaining wall. There in the darkness, high above the city lights, we prayed—for Mark, for healing, for a miracle from

God, but also for San Francisco. And when we drove back down the winding road from the peak, I didn't feel quite so alone.

Monday morning we went together to see Dr. Smoot, our general practitioner. He admitted there was much he didn't know about AIDS; Mark was his first personal case. But he summarized the basics of the disease, that it slowly broke down the body's immune system, making victims susceptible to a wide range of problems, two of the most common of which were pneumonia and Kaposi's sarcoma. He explained that KS was a type of lymphatic cancer, which, until the advent of AIDS, had been found only very rarely among elderly Mediterranean men. And no one yet knew why it seemed so prevalent among AIDS patients.

The doctor also mentioned a variety of experimental treatments available. And then he explained that the AIDS virus was most readily transmitted through sexual contact. Because I obviously had been exposed, he suggested an immediate blood test for me and a retesting for Mark. If I had not yet contracted the HIV virus, the only certain guarantee that I wouldn't get it from Mark in the future was sexual abstinence.

Finally the doctor warned us of the "social implications" of the disease. There were at the time some well-publicized cases of prejudice and persecution of AIDS patients around the United States. So he advised us, "Be careful who you tell!"

Shireen wanted to tell her folks everything right away. She had no doubts that everyone in her immediate family would be completely accepting, loving and supportive. Mark, with what was still a fairly short history with the Irvines, couldn't be so sure. So Shireen conceded. They would only tell her family what they told everyone else. That Mark had been diagnosed with a rare form of lymphatic cancer and his low white-blood-cell count was creating a blood-clotting problem. The truth, if not the whole truth.

The Ryans agreed to take their cues from Mark and Shireen, keeping the details in absolute confidence. Yet that was something of a courageous decision for Mike. With all the AIDS hysteria in the media at that time, parents' and citizens' groups around the country were demanding their rights to shelter their children or themselves from AIDS victims. So as a pastor, Mike faced the question of whether or not he had an ethical responsibility to inform his congregation, in case any members might wish to protect themselves from Mark. "To be perfectly honest," Mike said, "Donna and I were initially concerned about our own children. So I set out to learn everything I could in a crash course on AIDS. Everything I read, all the scientific evidence I found, all the experts I talked to, brought me to the same conclusion. AIDS is an infectious, but not contagious disease. Which meant casual contact with Mark presented no danger to my family or my congregation.

"I knew some people who knew Mark would probably have their suspicions. But I assured Mark and Shireen, 'It's up to you who you tell. And when you tell them.' "

The next person we told was a nutritionist friend of Mark's who had worked with a number of persons with AIDS. One Saturday, just over a week after the diagnosis, we stopped at the health food store on Market Street where Denise worked to ask her advice regarding diets being used to slow the progression of AIDS. She recommended some books so we could read up on a couple of diets. She also suggested a heavy regimen of vitamin therapy that had helped some of her clients. And she told us about a special public seminar sponsored by the San Francisco AIDS Foundation, which was to start a half hour later in a building only a few blocks down the street. "There will be doctors there from San Francisco General to talk about some of the most recent developments in AIDS treatment," she said.

Nearly two hundred people packed the meeting room when we slipped into a couple of the last seats. By the time the session started, people were standing along the walls. Most of the predominantly male crowd represented the gay community. I saw a handful of men in wheelchairs, others who bore the telltale purple lesions of KS on their bodies, and some whose faces had that drawn, gaunt look of poor health. Thinking how healthy Mark looked, I wondered how many of the other healthy-looking people in the audience also had AIDS.

Mark asked me to take notes, so I had to listen intently as a couple of different doctors took turns reporting on the latest treatments being used at SF General. A question-and-answer session followed in which the physicians fielded a wide range of questions—about the comparable side effects of radiation versus alpha-interferon treatments, rumors of progress with new chemotherapy, and the prospects for FDA approval of a number of experimental drugs now being used on AIDS patients in other countries. Mark and I both found the answers disheartening. The bottom line seemed to be that the medical community was groping in the dark for more effective treatments, none of which could promise any lasting success and many of which resulted in increased misery for those who subscribed to them.

On the way home, Mark reacted adamantly. "I'm not going to be blasted with radiation or chemo. And I don't ever want to go to General to be a human guinea pig for the latest experimental treatment! There has to be a better way." And he called to cancel an appointment he'd already had with one of the doctors who spoke at the seminar.

We decided to try a very strict candida yeast diet which cuts out dairy products, sugars and preservatives to concentrate on whole grains, fresh vegetables, and dishes containing fresh herbs. And we added megadoses of vitamins Mark's friend Denise had recommended. I joined Mark in his diet, but the effort was a three-times-daily reminder of the specter of AIDS.

My own tests came back with no indication of AIDS. Mark was probably more relieved than I was. Maybe it was naiveté, or just plain denial, but I had never been at all worried that I had it. However, just to be safe, we had made the decision to abstain from sexual intercourse after our first joint conference with the doctor.

Despite the drastic changes in our lifestyle, there continued to be a strong sense of unreality to the whole thing. In large part, this was because Mark still didn't seem seriously ill.

We talked and prayed a lot about divine healing. Mark said he felt certain that God was in the process of healing him. But all the signs indicated otherwise.

His toe continued to pain him greatly. More of the small purple KS lesions began appearing on Mark's body. Night sweats would keep him shivering for hours until the fever passed. His nose would bleed frequently, and his white-blood-cell count dropped dangerously low. Mark tired easily and began taking naps during the middle of the day; even then he didn't have the energy he needed to continue his former level of productivity.

The building in which Mark rented office space came up for sale that spring. So I encouraged him to move his office home. (The designer he'd hired the year before had decided to get married and left the company.) We had space enough in our front room for Mark and Michelle Fontaine, his assistant/office manager, to share an office. And I thought it'd be a plus for him to be right at home where he could relax and rest whenever he needed a break. Mark eventually agreed on the wisdom of moving his office home, but the decision didn't go down easily. For

him it seemed a major step backwards when he'd been so excited
the year before about his company's growing success.

Both he and Shireen agreed concessions had to be made with Mark's
business because he just didn't have the energy or stamina to push
for new clients or new jobs. But the Perrys were slow to make other
concessions. Mark pressed on with the projects he already had. The
two of them, but especially Shireen, learned all they could about
Mark's disease and the alternative treatments being used with AIDS
patients. Shireen read up on the macrobiotic diet and began combining some elements of that with the strict candida diet they were
already on. Mark began a regular routine of massages and acupres-
sure to relieve his pain.

The effort of thought and energy spent learning about and adjust-
ing to AIDS dominated their lives and their time over the next few
months. But in forcing them to focus on new routines of daily living,
it also kept them from thinking too much about the future. Each day
Mark remained the same, each new insight gained about AIDS, each
deliberate step taken to deal with the disease, gave reason to hope
and reason not to think six months down the road.

One of the highlights during those difficult months was an Oriental dinner party for eleven Mark and Shireen threw in honor of
Donna Ryan's and Pat Gabriel's (another friend) birthdays. Mark
transformed their house with the Far Eastern feel of Chinese lan-
terns and a Japanese paper fish kite. White Chinese laundry bags
accented with red bottoms and black Chinese lettering were stuffed
with pillows for seating at a low table. The group made sushi together,
and Mark and Shireen served miso soup, rice, stuffed salmon and
mandarin oranges.

Though the thought wasn't articulated, both Mark and Shireen
determined to continue to live their life together with as much en-
joyment and normality as possible. They even began working togeth-

er to design and create the costumes for a Christian theater's pro-
duction of "Godspell" scheduled later that summer.

In May, Mark and I spent a week alone at a friend's cabin in
the gold country of the Sierras. It felt so good to escape the
routine and the city just to rest, read, pray, explore and walk
together. And it was there, after three months of abstinence,
that we resumed our sex life. We'd discussed the issue with
doctors and made the decision we thought best for ourselves.
With the triple precautions of diaphragm, condoms and sper-
micidal gel, we felt any risk was very slight.

We knew some people would have made a different decision—
the only sure prevention being abstinence. But we felt our decision was best for us. While we'd learned to appreciate the intimacy of kissing and holding during our time of abstinence, we
came back from our time in the mountains feeling physically
reunited as husband and wife again.

Yet not everything was as it had been at the beginning of our
marriage. More and more of the household duties we'd always
done together fell to me. I did more of the cleaning, most of the
shopping, and eventually most of the meal planning. Mark
needed all the energy he could muster for his ongoing business
clients.

We did go sailing out in San Francisco Bay on the evening of
July fourth with my sister and brother-in-law, Marguerite and Ed.
We had a great view of the Oakland Coliseum fireworks. The
warm breeze and the spray of salt water acted as a tonic for our
minds and spirits. And we spent one special, relaxing July weekend up in the mountains with Mike and Donna Ryan and their
girls.

But the growing pressures of caring for Mark's needs, handling
the stresses of my own work, and continuing to hold potentially

supportive friends and loved ones off by our ongoing secrecy began to take their toll. The truth that I'd been denying by not facing could no longer be ignored.

One night I wrote this prayer: "Thank you, Lord, for helping me to finally realize my angry feelings. I'm carrying a burden on my shoulders that I want you to have. A burden for Mark's health and my life with Mark. I'm so tired."

Though Mark continued to talk just as much about how God was healing him, it became harder and harder for Shireen to echo the same assurances when all appearances belied his words. There's indication in Mark's journal that he no longer felt so sure of healing either. In late July he wrote, "Lord, I don't know what you have in store for me. But I'm yours. I love you. I praise you for every circumstance I'm in now."

And the tension he must have felt, between the faith he was expressing and the doubts he wasn't, began showing in his relationship with Shireen.

One day around the first of August, Mark had been to the doctor's, so I asked him about the appointment when I got home. He gave some short, vague answer. So I asked him for more specifics, and he exploded into a rage. I wasn't being supportive because I didn't really believe God was healing him. I didn't trust God. And I didn't trust him to know what the doctor said. I was always being a negative drain on his spirits and on and on.

I hadn't seen the tirade coming, and I felt helpless to do anything about it.

About this same time we'd heard about a controversial AIDS treatment being used in New York City by a Dr. Emanuel Rivici who had developed a chemical treatment which would directly attack cancer cells without the side effects of conventional chemotherapy. Dr. Rivici's program had its critics, but the technique had shown some success in breaking down the cancer cells of Kaposi's sarcoma.

So Mark called Dr. Rivici's Institute of Applied Biology and flew to New York as soon as he got an appointment. I wanted to go with him, but we decided I should save my vacation time so I could go with Mark to Hong Kong in September. Mark had been asked to take on another design project in Hong Kong by the same client who'd sent him to the Far East two years before.

Mark didn't respond to the therapy in New York as quickly as some patients had. So a planned one-week stay stretched to three weeks. Mark lost weight and became extremely weak. But the lesions finally began to heal. Once he had the dosage adjusted, the doctor provided an ongoing supply of medicine, and Mark came back home.

His weight loss and weakness alarmed me. But the lesions did look better. Mark felt healing had finally begun, and I hoped he was right. Heartened by this first real sign of improvement, Mark decided it was time to go public with our story. We talked to Mike Ryan, and he agreed to set aside an entire Sunday evening, September 8, 1985, for Mark to address the First Covenant congregation. Then we told my family the whole truth, and Mark was touched by their warm, accepting response.

The weekend prior to the scheduled church service, we celebrated our first anniversary with a variety of special activities. We listened to the tape of our wedding together. And we spent another relaxing afternoon together at the top of Mt. Tam, where we talked about our past and future.

Mark noted how the constant wind and bright sun had made most of the grass on the summit of Mt. Tam dry and brittle. But under a nearby oak tree, its gnarled branches hanging down almost to the ground, the sheltered grass remained lush, green and growing. Mark saw encouraging symbolism in that scene: just as the tree sheltered and protected the grass growing under its care, so God shelters and protects and gives vital life to those who grow close to him. That was the truth he wanted to share when he spoke before the church congregation.

Mark felt concerned about people's reaction when they found out he had AIDS. But I supported his determination to go through with the service at church. I think we both sensed it would be a turning point in our ordeal.

But we never suspected the way our lives were to turn.

CHAPTER SIX

*T*HE SUNDAY MORNING BULLETIN OF
the First Covenant Church of San Francisco for September 8, 1985,
invited everyone to come back that night for "A Gathering of the
King's Family"—an evening with Mark Perry. Almost two hundred
people packed out the church's downstairs fellowship hall. Most who
came were members of the church. But Shireen's family was there,
as were a number of Mark's old friends whom he had invited from
the gay community.

After a time of singing, Mike Ryan turned the microphone over
to Mark, who very briefly summarized his physical problems of the
previous year; talked about tests, the biopsy; and then said, "On
March 8 of this year, I was sitting in a hematologist's office and

was pronounced to have six months to live. I was diagnosed with a terminal cancer called Kaposi's sarcoma, the result of something called the HIV virus. What this means is that I have what is referred to as the Acquired Immune Deficiency Syndrome, or AIDS."

The quiet room fell totally silent. Mike Ryan returned to the microphone to summarize the current knowledge on AIDS and to read a brief medical description of the syndrome before Mark continued his talk and admitted the truth that only a few people in the room had known. He said, "Prior to my life in Christ . . . I lived a homosexual lifestyle, exclusively, in the homosexual community. I had homosexual relationships, so there's no question as to how or why I would be susceptible.

"But four years ago on Christmas Day, I met Jesus Christ, and I asked him to take control of my life. And at that point I was delivered of the lie and deception of believing that I was born and created to be a homosexual. Christ healed me of past memories and habits, of mannerisms, and he's blessed me with a beautiful wife and an incredible relationship with her. This new life I have received is a miracle in itself. I recognize that. And I praise God for that."

Mark admitted his fear of publicly admitting his past to the congregation. And he talked about how hard it had been the previous few months not being able to share his burden with the people who'd come to mean so much to him.

At that point Mark motioned me to come to the microphone to share an insight I'd had during a quiet time of Bible reading and praying a few months before. As I looked out over that room of attentive, friendly faces, I told about reading the story of Daniel and how some of his enemies had tricked King Darius into passing a law prohibiting prayer to God, a law they knew Daniel, one of the king's favorite officials, wouldn't obey. Then they turned Daniel in and demanded his death as the law required. But when the king had reluctantly punished Daniel by throwing him into the lion's den, the Lord protected him. And when he walked out safely, the king had Daniel's enemies cast in to be devoured.

"Afterwards," I said, "King Darius wrote this letter to all the people in the land: 'I issue a decree that in every part of my kingdom people must fear and reverence the God of Daniel. "For he is a living God and he endures forever; his kingdom will not be destroyed, his dominion will never end. He rescues and he saves; he performs signs and wonders in the heavens and on the earth. He has rescued Daniel from the power of the lions." ' "

At that point, I looked up from my Bible at the people gathered in the church basement. "As a result of reading this passage," I told them, "It was confirmed in my heart that I was sure the Lord was going to do signs and wonders in Mark's life. But I also knew before that could happen, Mark would have to share his past life and share the details of the illness he was going through with the congregation and with other people in the community. And this night has brought that about."

As I started back to my seat, Mark whispered a reminder in my ear, and I stepped again to the mike. "One last thing in relation to this. My constant prayer is that the Lord will give Mark endurance and strength. But my prayer that day—a prayer I prayed only once and then just trusted God to answer—was: 'Lord, just as your angels shut the lions' mouths, please shut the hunger of the cancer cells. Kill the cancer cells with your power, just as the lions killed Daniel's adversaries.'

"And then the question: 'Do more people need to know about Mark's illness before you can be glorified, as the king glorified you and proclaimed you to his nation?' "

A wave of applause rolled around the room as Shireen returned to her chair. Mark shared some other Scriptures and some songs that had been especially meaningful to him. And then he read the story in Acts 3 about Peter and John healing the crippled man at the gate of the temple. He read about the peoples' reaction and Peter's chastisement: "Men of Israel, why does this surprise you? . . . By faith in the name of Jesus, this man whom you see and know was made strong. It is Jesus' name and the faith that comes through him that has given this complete healing to him, as you can all see. . . . Repent, then, and turn to God, so that your sins may be wiped out, that times of refreshing may come from the Lord."

Finally, Mark challenged those in attendance to examine their own lives and get rid of whatever was keeping them separated from God. And he added, "You are my friends and family, and I love you."

When Mark finished, Mike Ryan reclaimed the microphone to remind everyone that God had already forgotten Mark's past, "so we should too." Then he called Shireen and a couple of other people to come forward and put their hands on Mark as everyone else gathered around holding hands. "No longer is this a burden Mark has to carry alone," Mike said, and the group surrounded Mark with prayer.

One of Mark's old friends from the gay lifestyle voiced the reaction of many people there in the service when he said, "I can sense the love of God in this church tonight." Others who were there remember it as "a moving, inspiring service" and "a powerful testimony to the love of God's family."

After the service, so many people crowded around to hug each of us and express their love and support that Mark and I went home that night feeling more encouraged than we had any night since his diagnosis. Now that others knew Mark had AIDS, I felt renewed hope that God could bring real glory to himself by healing Mark. And Mark, who had feared rejection by the church, was nearly ecstatic with joy at the warm, loving acceptance he'd received, from the group as a whole and from so many individuals who had stayed to express their love and support after the service. I think we both felt a true freedom in the realization that other people could now help shoulder the load we'd silently been carrying for so many months.

On Monday Mark told me he was feeling the power of people praying for him. He said his lesions would be gone by Wednesday and he would be healed. He awakened me early Tuesday morning to say the Lord had told him he no longer needed the medicine he'd gotten from Dr. Rivici, so he'd thrown it all away.

Wednesday night we ate dinner with a friend who also had AIDS. Mark seemed strangely adamant in his advice to Sean about what he should or shouldn't do in the way of treatment.

> Though his body was slowing down, Mark's mind seemed to be shifting into overdrive. He dictated a long list of ideas to Michelle, his office manager, about how they could expand his design business to become a successful international company. "Some of his thoughts seemed absolutely brilliant," Michelle said. "Others were really off the wall." Citing his weakness, he told Michelle she would have to become president of his international company and execute his design ideas. "He even proposed doubling my salary immediately," Michelle said. "But I was the one who kept the books, so I knew that was impossible. I just wrote down the ideas he came out with and later threw most of my notes away."

On Friday Mark seemed to lose all sense of hunger or thirst. He ate and drank so little that Michelle (who was with him all day) and I were both alarmed. By Friday night he was so weak he said he couldn't walk from the bedroom to the bathroom. I had to get a desk chair with wheels from the office in the front room and roll him to the bathroom. Helping him onto the toilet I felt suddenly very afraid that he could die before the night was over.

He seemed so quiet and unresponsive, as if he were in his own world. I'd never seen him so lifeless and withdrawn.

> Unbeknownst to Shireen, Mark had awakened in the middle of the previous night and placed several long-distance phone calls to several of his family members and friends, requesting that they please come to First Covenant Church on Sunday morning because "something important is going to happen." Mark had asked Mike Ryan if he could speak to the church during the service, and Mike had cautiously agreed to let him take a couple of minutes.
>
> After the wonderfully positive response the previous Sunday evening, Mark was convinced God had given him another special message to share with the church. And that God was going to perform a miracle of healing in the Sunday service.

By Saturday I had a terrible feeling of fear in the pit of my stomach. I knew Mark was no longer himself. He was sharing Bible verses with me that just didn't fit the interpretation he wanted to give them. He began talking about his plans for Sunday with an almost messianic attitude that terrified me. His behavior seemed so irrational, I feared he would make a fool of himself and discredit the wonderful testimony he'd given just the week before.

Mark's mother, Mary, brother Bruce and sister Barbara arrived Saturday in response to his calls. Mary and Barbara stayed overnight with my parents in Oakland. Bruce stayed with us and volunteered to chauffeur us to church the next morning. Mike Ryan had asked that we arrive a half hour ahead of time to discuss what Mark wanted to share. But Mark, who dressed completely in white, dawdled around so long we didn't get away from home until minutes before the service was to start.

I sat in the back seat with Mark as Bruce drove. "Bruce!" Mark snapped at one point. "Can't you please drive a little gentler.

Maybe you could drive around just one of the potholes and not try to hit every bump in the street!"

We didn't arrive at church until five minutes before the service started. Mike had already taken his place up front. Yet, just a little ways into the service, Mike announced: "Mark Perry has a short word he'd like to share with us this morning."

I walked down the aisle with Mark to lend him support. I stood beside him as he began to read a passage from Revelation that began with the words, "I, John." I winced as he inserted his own name and read, "I, John Mark." The moment he stopped reading, before Mark could say anything, Mike stepped beside him, put his arm around Mark's shoulder and asked everyone to pray with him for Mark. As Mike prayed, Mark's arms and legs began to twitch and then he began to shake violently. He leaned his head against Mike's shoulder, his knees buckled, and he fainted right on the spot. Mike tightened his grip on Mark's shoulder, finished his prayer, and in a single motion swept Mark up in his arms as if he were a limp rag doll and carried him right out of the sanctuary. Mark regained consciousness a few minutes later on a couch in an adjoining church room. I sat with him there until the end of the service when a number of people sought us out to express their concern for Mark.

That next week was when we had our reservations to go to Hong Kong. I'd been trying to talk Mark into canceling our tickets, but he'd angrily insisted he was going to be strong enough to go and that I wasn't showing enough faith in God's healing.

On Tuesday I took him to our physician in hopes the doctor could talk Mark out of the Hong Kong trip. Dr. Smoot called Dr. Rivici in New York, and they both strongly advised against making the trip. Still Mark refused to let me cancel the tickets.

The doctor privately indicated to me he thought Mark needed

some kind of psychiatric treatment. I was afraid he was right; but I didn't know how to convince Mark he needed help.

His behavior became more bizarre by the day. He began "re-organizing" the house; pulling everything out in a room and then going on to another project without finishing what he'd started. He went on a cleaning-and-pitching spree, throwing stuff away by the garbage-bag full. One day his brother Bruce, who was still staying with us, salvaged our passports and the deed to our house which were on their way to the neighbor's dumpster across the street.

I came home another day to discover that Mark had complete-ly reorganized my clothes—by color. Not sweaters here, under-wear in this drawer, socks over there. Not even by outfit. Just by color. Every item of pink clothing here. Greens there. And not just by color, but in order of the color spectrum—from yellow green to blue green. And folded a certain way. Underwear into thirds. Socks folded this way. Sweaters just so. As I listened to him proudly explain his weird new system, I just wanted to cry in frustration.

One day at lunch, Michelle found Mark in the kitchen, eating a hard-boiled egg, shell and all. Another afternoon, when I came home in the afternoon and Michelle tried to pull me aside to fill me in on some of the things Mark had done that day, he blew up and accused us of conspiring against him. And on Friday, September 20, only days after offering to double Michelle's salary immediately and make her president of "Masterplan Internation-al," he fired her. He was giving her a warm good-by hug when I walked in from work. It didn't make any sense. And he wouldn't even try to explain why to Michelle or to me.

Because I wasn't supportive of his decision, Mark got angry and didn't want me around that night, so I agreed to use the evening to visit my sister Ronah who'd had her first baby the day before. Bruce stayed with Mark, and I spent the night at my parents'.

Mark called me at my folks' house the next day to accuse me of not appreciating his organization or help around home. He complained I wasn't trusting him anymore. And he demanded my full cooperation as my husband and head of our house. He expected me to leave everything in order as he had put it. "And if you don't want to cooperate," he said, "you don't need to come home or to be married to me!"

I returned Sunday to find all the kitchen shelves completely reorganized and a huge salad bowl in which Mark was soaking every bean in the house. A few days later I came home from work to find the beans had all disappeared; I had no idea where.

The day before our scheduled flight to the Far East, I canceled our tickets without telling Mark. I didn't say anything the next day, I just never packed. Mark was furious.

Thursday morning, the twenty-sixth, Mark belligerently instructed me as to what I should wear to work. And when I got home that afternoon, he scolded me for "rushing into the house," saying, "if you want a pleasant evening, you better slow down and cooperate." I told him I didn't understand what it was he wanted. And in the ensuing argument he declared he didn't care about me, and I obviously didn't care about him anymore.

Friday Bruce went away for the weekend, and Mark was home alone that day. I walked into the house after work to find the kitchen a mess, a scorched pan on the stove, the house filled with the smell of burning plastic. And Mark asleep in bed, oblivious to the world.

I cleaned up enough to start a spaghetti supper. When Mark awakened he suggested we work on my wardrobe. When I didn't

enthusiastically embrace the idea, he got mad and stormed into
the bathroom and I went on fixing supper. When the meal was
ready he still hadn't come out of the bathroom, so I opened the
door to check on him. He was standing in front of the mirror,
cutting his hair. He'd already shaved off most of his full beard.

"Mark, what are you doing?" I asked. "You just had a haircut."
He began to rant and rave so loudly our next-door neighbor
Dave Smith-Walsh heard the ruckus and came over to see what
was wrong. Mark wouldn't talk and he said he wasn't hungry
either. So Dave went back home, and I ate my spaghetti alone
and went directly to bed.

"I awakened to the bell of the microwave at 4:30 in the morning. Realizing Mark wasn't in bed with me, I got up to investigate.
I found him sitting at the table, eating warmed-up spaghetti. He'd
shaved his head. The only hair remaining above his shoulders
was a small goatee.

The next evening Mark and Shireen went to a play their neighbor
and friend Amy Smith-Walsh was directing across the bay. But Mark
couldn't sit through the performance. He slipped out into the lobby
and paced back and forth, mumbling to himself.

A number of friends came to the play, including Mike and Donna
Ryan. Shireen was glad other people could witness some of Mark's
strange behavior; maybe someone could help her understand it. She
felt certain Mark was on the verge of an emotional breakdown, but
she also felt that part of the problem must be a strong spiritual
oppression.

Both may have been true. But Shireen didn't know there was a
third possible factor: one of the now commonly recognized symptoms of AIDS is an extreme pattern of paranoia, irrationality or
bizarre behavior. Mark exhibited all three.

Sunday night Mark accused me of not being the wife I was supposed to be and refused to sleep in bed with me. I rose early Monday morning to find him lying awake on the trundle bed in our guest room. He seemed surprised I was up so early, and as he hurriedly got out of bed he told me he planned to leave that morning. To take a trip.

"But Mark," I argued, "you're not strong enough to go anywhere alone. You're just not healthy."

He insisted he was. So while he got dressed I called Dave next door and asked him to please come and talk Mark out of leaving. But when Dave showed up at the door, Mark became livid at his interference. When Mark stormed back into the bathroom, I hid his car keys. He came out a few minutes later and began a frantic, furious search for his keys.

"If you just tell me where you're going," I said, "I'll give you back your keys."

Mark exploded into another rage and then bolted out the front door and down the steps. A few moments later I heard his car start. It had been unlocked, and Mark kept an extra ignition key in the car.

I ran to the door, but by the time I got outside Mark was driving away. And I had no idea where he was heading or if he was strong enough to get there.

CHAPTER SEVEN

I RUSHED BACK INTO THE HOUSE THINK-
ing, *What do I do? Who do I call? How do I stop him?* And on the
table in our dining area I found his note saying, "I have to get
away for a few days. I'll be back."

That made me feel better. He'd evidently written the note the
night before and had planned to leave before I awakened. That
meant he'd at least thought about where he was going and what
he was going to do. Sure enough, his suitcase was gone and
some of his clothes. At least he'd made some provision. *Maybe
he'll be okay.*

But in the next few minutes of pacing around the house and
looking for some clue as to where he was going, I discovered

he'd taken more than clothes. Our silver flatware was gone. So were some of Mark's favorite brass pieces. A quick inventory revealed our TV wasn't in the closet and a number of Mark's special mementos had been taken as well.

If what he said in the note was true, that he was planning to come back in a few days, the things he took didn't make any sense. But then a lot of things he'd done lately didn't make much sense. Not knowing what to think, I began to worry again.

No word came all that day. Or the next. Finally, on the third day, the call came. *It's Mark! He's okay!* He called to tell me he was fine, but when I asked where he was, he refused to say "because you hid my car keys." I told him I was worried and asked him again to please tell me where he was. Still he refused. He angrily accused me of smothering him and failing to be a support to him, and he said he needed to be away for a while. I apologized and told him I accepted his wanting to get away, but that I had to know where he was. I begged him to tell me, and I could almost hear the spite in his voice when he refused and said he'd call again in a few days. Then he hung up. And I cried and prayed: "Lord, protect him. And show me what to do!"

Two nights later I awakened crying from a nightmare. The clock beside the bed read 1:20 A.M. And the terrible thought that I couldn't shake was *What if Mark dies alone?* What if he dies out there somewhere and I never see him again? What if he dies still angry at me and I can't tell him again how much I love him?

Lying there in the darkness, crying, I begged God not to let Mark die without me.

Days of worry passed liked decades. I'd never in my life felt so helpless or so afraid. At last he called. The anger still evident in his voice, he said he wanted me to send his car keys to his mother.

"Is that where you are now?" I asked. When he wouldn't answer, I said, "I miss you. And I want you to know I love you."

He told me he was feeling better. That he was doing some painting and sculpting. He suggested a couple projects I could ask his brother Bruce to do around our house. And he asked me again to send his keys to his mother's house—that she'd make sure he got them. (The implication was that he wasn't there.)

"I promise I'll send you the keys," I assured him. "But I'm worried about you. Won't you please tell me where you are?"

He told me he would hang up if I wasn't willing to keep the conversation positive. I promised I would. And then I heard a click . . . *NO!* . . . and the dreadful silence of a dead line. He'd hung up anyway! I felt devastated.

I tried to call Mark back the rest of that week. Either the phone would just ring, or his mother, Mary, would answer and say that Mark didn't want to talk to me. She would say very little, even in response to my questions about Mark's health. Finally, a week or so after Mark got to Oregon, she did say that Mark was scheduled for surgery the next day to have the lump removed from the back of his head and that, no, Mark didn't want me to come up to be with him.

The surgeon successfully removed the benign tumor from the back of Mark's head, relieving the pressure the growth had been exerting on one of the main arteries to his brain. The immediate physical relief also seemed to improve Mark's mental and emotional state; he had a brief, but mostly positive, phone conversation with Shireen. And though he didn't respond, Shireen sent him a number of letters, assuring him of her love, and her desire to do whatever she needed to do and make whatever changes she needed to make, so that he could come home. She let him know that his many friends were concerned about him and that she'd only told them Mark was out of town visiting his mom and she didn't have many details to report about his health. Shireen wanted to be sure Mark didn't think she was criticizing him to friends or that people were gossiping about his leaving. She desperately wanted to avoid saying or doing anything that might create a barrier to Mark's return.

One day a close friend asked how Shireen would feel if Mark died in Oregon. Shireen had not wanted to face that question. The answer was angry!—at Mark. And probably even at God for not stopping it all from happening.

In the meantime, the primary feelings were loneliness and fear. And more than three long weeks passed.

On October 22, I left work a few minutes early and stopped by the post office to mail another letter to Mark. I was still a block away from home when I spotted a rental truck backed into our drive. That sight hadn't really registered before I also saw Mary, Mark's mother, descending our front steps, carrying a cardboard box.

What is going on? The answer to that thought should have been clear by the time I pulled to the curb and parked in front of our neighbor's house. But I couldn't believe it.

"What are you doing?" I asked Mary the second I jumped out of my car. Mark's aunt was there too.

Mary answered that she was just doing what Mark wanted her to do.

Mark's here! He must be! Where? The truck was almost full of our household possessions. They were about to leave; no doubt they'd planned to get away before I returned home. *Mark's about to leave again!* I had to stop him; I had to have help.

I charged up the steps and into the office just inside the open front door. I grabbed the phone to call Mike Ryan, but both the phone directory and the church directory were gone. *I have the number in my purse. In the car.* I dashed back out the door and down the steps. And there was Mark! By the truck.

"Mark! What are you doing?"

He looked at me and coldly replied, "I have nothing to say to you."

"Mark, I'm your wife. Please tell me what's going on!" Without another word, he turned to head back alongside the house.

What do I do? I have to have help! I grabbed my purse and raced back up the steps to call Mike. He wasn't at his office.

Outside, the big sliding back door of the truck slammed shut. I dropped the phone and sprinted back down the steps to the street. Mark was walking toward the passenger's side of the cab; I ran in front of him and he stopped.

"Mark, what are you doing?"

"I'm taking my things," he said.

"They're *our* things," I responded.

He didn't say anything to that. He merely shoved me aside and climbed into the cab. Before I could stop him, he slammed the door, catching my sweater in the process. His aunt started the truck as I tugged at my sweater. I slipped the sweater free of the door as she shifted into gear and slowly pulled off down the street.

I ran inside to try to call Mike Ryan at home. Donna answered. Mike wasn't there, but Donna already knew what was happening because our next-door neighbor Amy had come home a few minutes before me and had tried to call Mike when she realized what was going on.

Donna suggested I call a police sergeant friend of the Ryans to ask if there was any way to prevent Mark from leaving town with our things. I'd noted the license plate of the truck; it would be easy enough to spot crossing one of the bridges out of the Bay Area.

Sergeant Pat told me it was a civil dispute, not a criminal dispute, so the police couldn't stop Mark from leaving. But he talked with me for almost an hour about the details and recommended I get some counseling for myself. "In a situation like this," he said, "it's even more traumatic for you than it is for your husband. You really need to seek professional help."

I thanked him for his concern. I did appreciate his compassion. But the terrible truth remained: my dying husband was gone again. And from all appearances, this time he didn't plan to return.

I walked through the house in a state of shock. The office still contained a desk, some bookshelves and most of Mark's business books and records. The living room was bare; the sectional, the Chinese wedding basket and lamps were all gone. They'd cleared out the dining room furniture. The bedroom looked like a disaster area with my clothes scattered on the bare floor where the drawers of our large tansu chest had been emptied before the chest was carried out. Our bed was gone, along with the smaller tansu nightstand. All that remained in the guest bedroom was the trundle bed my aunt had given us.

I walked into the kitchen to find bare shelves. Gone were a majority of the pots and pans, the small appliances and most of the cutlery. What remained were a couple of cups, one plate, and a single setting of stainless steel.

I felt as if I were walking around in a nightmare. The reality seemed impossible to accept—that I'd been rejected, abandoned and betrayed by the one I loved more than anyone else in the world. I stood in our empty house and cried.

I tried to call Mark several times over the following few days. But he didn't want to talk. So I finally wrote him another letter. (Though Mark had yet to answer any of the letters I'd written in the month he'd been gone.) I told him: "My love is too deep to intentionally hurt you. But I feel hurt and left out of your life."

For several days in a row, I received no mail of any kind. But I was too distraught to think about the implication. Until the end of the month approached and I realized I hadn't gotten even the routine monthly bills. I called the telephone company to find out that they were planning to terminate service the next day if the bill wasn't paid. When I got a similar response from the utilities company, I checked with the post office to learn that Mark had filled out the forms to have all our mail forwarded to Oregon.

When I called Mark to find out what was going on, he agreed I should go to the post office and specify only mail for "Mark Perry" should be forwarded. My mail should be delivered. He also agreed I should have any household accounts such as the utilities and phone transferred to my name.

But Mark spent most of that phone conversation criticizing me. For not being a supportive wife. For not believing he was being healed. For not emotionally leaving my family and cleaving to him when we had gotten married. For running up a huge long-distance phone bill when he'd been in New York for treatment back in August. For ruining his friendships by not wanting to socialize more. For not wanting a dog. For never wanting to go out to eat, but staying home all the time. . . . And the list went on.

As the days and weeks passed, I became more and more discouraged, with no idea what was going on in Mark's mind or with his family up in Oregon. I worried briefly that he'd file for legal separation and I'd never see him again before he died. But when I confessed that fear one day to Michelle, she assured me that she and the handful of others who knew what Mark had done were praying with me and believing he would return. But it wasn't easy to consistently believe that.

Despite her sagging confidence, in one of her letters to Mark, Shireen wrote: "At our wedding I vowed to be with you in sickness or in health, for richer or for poorer, and I want you to know I'm keeping that vow. I'm waiting and . . . I have our home ready for your return."

There wasn't much to keep ready. She slept on the trundle bed Mark had left. A friend brought over a rocker and a reading lamp. She covered the second trundle mattress, and decorated it with a few cushions she made out of scrap material and leftover batting she'd found in the basement; that served as her living room couch. But other than that, she deliberately decided not to try to furnish the house; she wanted there to be room for all their possessions when Mark returned.

She obviously didn't do much entertaining. And only a few of her closest friends knew what had happened (and they were asked to keep it in strictest confidence, even though they were pretty upset at Mark for what he'd done). Shireen didn't want many people to know the full story, in large part to protect Mark from others' judgments and to avoid raising any feelings of resentment or embarrassment that might be a barrier to his return.

Yet his departure created numerous problems for Shireen. She had to find design business details in his office records when clients called to ask questions. She took a day off work just to get the details sorted out with the post office and the utilities. And the worst was yet to come.

One day, walking into the house after work, I stooped to pick up the mail inside the door. Shuffling through it, I noticed three pieces from my credit union. Thinking that was odd, I opened one. It said I had an overdraft in my credit union checking account. And it listed three checks. *Impossible,* I thought, ripping open the second envelope. More overdrafts. *There's got to be some mistake.* The third envelope contained more of the same. In all, ten checks had bounced for a total overdraft of just over two thousand dollars. I couldn't believe it.

As I stood staring at the statements, I noticed the check numbers. They were higher than any of the numbered checks I'd written. Suddenly I realized what had happened, and a quick look at the box of checks in the office confirmed my suspicions; Mark had taken a supply of checks from the bottom of the box so I wouldn't notice them.

In frustration, I called and asked him to please tell me what checks he'd written so I could know what was happening with our account. He refused to say. So I closed our joint account, opened one in my name and put a stop payment on all his outstanding checks. The next time I talked to him on the phone, Mark was furious about what I'd done, but I didn't see that I had any choice.

I was getting sick and tired of untangling Mark's messes. Some days my frustration and discouragement gave way to anger. Until I began daily praying, "Lord, don't let bitterness grow in me."

Without God's strength, bitterness on my part could have become an insurmountable barrier. Mark certainly seemed full of bitterness. Whenever he would condescend to talk with me on the phone, he complained that I was being irresponsible, I needed to grow up and be an independent woman, that I didn't respect his authority in our marriage and that I didn't trust him.

The longer his accusations went on, the more I began to wonder if there was something to them. If maybe I was to blame for his leaving. But when I expressed those self-doubts to Mike Ryan, he assured me, "That's just not true, Shireen. This isn't your problem, it's Mark's."

But one thing Mark accused me of was true. It *was* hard to trust a man whose messes I continued to find as the weeks passed. Like the beans he'd soaked and planted that were now coming up all over our back yard like a jungle. Or like the tool box I discovered inexplicably buried under a compost heap in the corner of the back-yard garden; when I opened it I found it full of putrid, rotting garbage and crawling with maggots.

Things like that reminded me that Mark had been a very sick man before he left. But that realization was hardly a comfort when he was so far away, and I had no real clue as to his current health—physically, emotionally or spiritually. All I could do was pray. That God would forgive any of my failures that might have contributed to Mark's leaving. That God would open Mark's eyes to see whatever deception was going on in his mind. That God would destroy any barriers between us and loose Mark from the powers of anger and depression that seemed to be destroying him and our marriage.

It was those daily, deliberate, spiritual warfare-type prayers that helped me maintain my own hope and sanity. In the face of my helplessness, praying became an action I could take.

Yet Shireen also struggled to keep the lines of communication open with Mark. When he wouldn't talk on the phone, she wrote letters. She read books on communication and tried to put the principles she read about into practice. Once, after Mark complained that her letters didn't sound like her, she voiced her thoughts into a tape recorder and then, replaying the tape, she tried to translate the patterns of her spoken speech into a written letter. The process took her hours, but she was willing to go to any lengths to communicate.

During one conversation Mark instructed me to investigate the feasibility of renting out the house to ease our tightening financial crunch. He even suggested two businessmen friends who could advise me on how to do it. But both men agreed that even if I rented the house for more than the mortgage payments, the rent I'd have to pay to live anywhere else would more than cancel out the gains. When I gave Mark the verdict, he complained that I'd given up too easily and hadn't really wanted to follow through with his idea.

When he would talk with me, Mark continued to complain about everything. The strict diet *I'd* had him on—even though it had been a joint decision. The lack of medical help he'd found in San Francisco. The lack of understanding and support from the church. That the people he thought were his friends didn't care about him. That I only cared about my own world. Most of the time, I just listened to his rantings, choosing not to argue for fear he'd get angry and hang up. Any continuing contact, even negative contact, seemed better than none.

Along in November, Donna Ryan and I, plus a couple of other friends of Mark's, cooked up an idea. We decided to get together a bunch of Mark's closest friends and record messages to send to Oregon to let him know people did care. Pat and Paul Gabriel, a couple who'd come to Mark's regular Bible study, volunteered to host the gathering at their home.

That evening, after dinner, fifteen of the Perrys' friends went one at a time into a back room at the Gabriel's to record a personal message to Mark. Some were stern, some were tearful, all of them told Mark how much they missed him and how much they loved him.

Paul Gabriel said, ". . . somehow we've failed to communicate or you've failed to believe we really love you, Mark. . . . It's time for you to get your butt back down here and see that there's more love for you here in San Francisco than anywhere this side of eternity."

Dave and Amy Smith-Walsh, the next-door neighbors who had both become Christians as a result of Mark's influence, thanked him for the faith he'd introduced them to and talked about how much they missed him. Mike Ryan filled him in on church doings and expressed how much he missed Mark. Donna Ryan tearfully reassured Mark of her love and her desire to see him again soon.

A little more than halfway through the hour-long tape, after ten other people had shared, Shireen recorded a brief message. She offered a two-sentence report on the party going on in the next room before saying, "I do miss you, Mark. I love you. And I'd like to be able to give you a great big warm hug."

Holt Satterfield, another friend of Mark's, expressed his love and respect by telling Mark, "You are my mentor . . . the person I looked to as a seeker of wisdom and truth." He said he didn't understand why Mark was in Oregon but that there was a "whole roomful of people gathered for you. . . . I'm praying for you. Tons of people are praying . . ."

And Michelle Fontaine, the assistant Mark had fired back in September, told him how much she missed him. Then with her guitar for accompaniment, she sang two songs for Mark which she'd written years before in a time when she'd been struggling. The first was a haunting number called "Darkness" and the second, about God's grace and provision, she'd titled, "Your Love for Me."

The next time I called Mark, he told me he'd listened to the tape. He appreciated all the encouraging things everyone had said.

Everyone but me, that is. He complained that I'd had "nothing, nothing at all to say."

My husband was sick, maybe dying—hundreds of miles away from me. Yet no matter what I did to try to communicate my love, it never seemed to be enough.

CHAPTER EIGHT

*S*OMEHOW GOD GAVE ME THE GRACE to be patient. I was even able to write Mark to say: "I'm trying to be a good wife. I won't abandon you. When you get well enough to come home, I'll be waiting."

Later I wrote to ask Mark his Thanksgiving plans and to say I'd be glad to come to Portland or meet him somewhere else for a couple of days. I told him I thought we needed a chance to be together and talk. And that I missed him.

He never responded to my questions or my suggestions. So it was hard to be thankful that Thanksgiving. We'd talked the year before about our mutual desire to establish our own holiday traditions for Thanksgiving and Christmas, and now Mark wasn't even with me to share Thanksgiving Day.

Despite my constant prayers, the prospects for having him home for Christmas didn't seem any better. So I agreed to let a friend, who was being transferred out of San Francisco, store her furniture at my house for the month, or until she found a place to live in Utah where she was moving. No longer greeted by empty rooms when I got home each night, I began to feel like it was a home again, and not just a house on hold.

I needed all the comfort and normality I could get that winter. Not only had Mark's absence dragged on and on with no noticeable change in his angry attitude toward me, but my family received the devastating word that Ronah and Barry's three-month-old boy, Braden, had a very rare, incurable blood disorder. His white-blood-cell count had not been good since birth, but the results of a new test identified the problem as Familial Erythrophagocytic Lymphohistiocytosis (FEL). Though there were some long-term survivors, the doctors said the prognosis was poor in young children. They wouldn't say how long they thought Braden would live, because they just didn't know.

Once again I was confronted with the specter of terminal illness. And little Braden's tragic situation became another constant, painful reminder that nine months had passed since Mark's doctor gave him six months to live. However many months he now had left, I longed to spend them with him.

Maybe the Christmas holidays, the celebration of Christ's birth, and the anniversary of Mark's own rebirth as a Christian would provide the opportunity for me to finally break through to Mark, to persuade him of my love. I could only hope. And pray.

One day while in prayer I asked God to give me an idea for

a Christmas present, something that would not just please Mark, but convincingly symbolize for him my love and my commitment to do whatever he thought necessary before we could be reunited. As I prayed, a vivid image came to my mind. I pictured a dog bounding across a room and leaping into Mark's arms.

Mark had wanted a dog since soon after we were married. But my feeling about pets was that animals are usually more bother than they're worth. We both worked; we liked to live our lives and plan our days spontaneously. Locking ourselves into the responsibilities of pet ownership just didn't seem practical. So we hadn't done it.

The prospect still didn't appeal to me. But the picture I had in my mind of Mark and a dog was so clear, so out of character with my own thoughts, that I felt convinced the idea was from God—his answer to my prayer about a Christmas gift. *Okay,* I told the Lord, reluctantly. *But Mark has always wanted a miniature Schnauzer, so it has to be a Schnauzer. We don't have any money to spend, so it'll have to be free. And I'm not up to training a puppy, so this dog has to be housebroken.* I figured if the Lord could provide all that, who was I to resist the idea?

But I didn't wait for an angel to show up at my door with a Schnauzer on the end of a leash. I checked with the local SPCA to see if they had any Schnauzers. They didn't. So I left my name, hoping to get a call from them before Christmas.

With the holiday fast approaching, I decided I had to have a back-up gift, in case the dog idea didn't work out. I sewed Mark a new chef's apron, and I bought him a wallet. I wrapped those two gifts and mailed them to Portland a few days before Christmas, along with two belts I'd made for Mark's mom and his sister.

A couple days later a package came for me from Mark. My

friends Pat and Laurice were with me right after I picked it up from the post office. They urged me to open it and the gift-wrapped package inside. So I did. Mark had sent me a little make-up case, and he'd bought me a wallet too. I can't say I appreciated the irony at the time—a husband and wife in ever-deepening financial straits giving each other new, empty wallets. Though encouraged by the fact that Mark had at least sent a gift, his present troubled me. The wallet was just not of a quality or of the workmanship Mark would ordinarily choose. It made me wonder whether he just hadn't cared, or whether his health had deteriorated more than he'd let on.

I spent Christmas Day celebrating with my family at my folks' house. Christmas afternoon I psyched myself up to place a phone call to Portland. While I longed to talk to Mark on Christmas, I dreaded his ranting criticisms which had typified every conversation we'd had since he left. Christmas without Mark and with my family (including the only grandchild, Braden) had been emotional enough without a nasty, negative exchange with Mark.

Mark's mom answered the phone. When I wished her a Merry Christmas and asked to speak to Mark, she went to see if he wanted to talk. A few seconds later, Mark came on. I told him Merry Christmas and thanked him for his gift. I also explained where I was and that everyone in my family wanted a chance to send their greetings. So he talked briefly with Dad, Mom, each of my siblings and the in-laws. Everyone expressed love and concern and told Mark they missed him and wished he was with us. Ronah gave him an update on Braden's condition, and after Mark asked her a few questions about the baby's treatment, he told Ronah the chemotherapy his Oregon doctor had prescribed was very similar to Braden's. I stayed on an extension the entire time; in all his exchanges with my family, Mark sounded cordial and warm—just like his old self.

Finally it was just the two of us on the line again. He seemed more reserved and less expressive with me than he had with anyone else. And he did offer a couple of brief complaints: saying he'd left because I'd been smothering him and I just didn't exhibit common sense—a new charge evidenced by the old gripe about the exorbitant phone bill when I'd called him so many times in New York. But all in all, that was the most civil communication we'd had since Mark left home in September. He even told me he loved me before we hung up, the first I'd heard those words from my love's lips in months.

So Christmas turned out to be a happy day after all.

Early in January, Mark phoned me. Another first. He made some of the same old complaints, but the words didn't seem as harsh. I could sense it more than I could explain it—but there seemed to be a subtle change in Mark. I prayed and prayed and prayed that the softening would continue.

The second week in January a man called to say the SPCA had given him my number as someone who wanted a Schnauzer. His dog was eight years old, housebroken, and he wanted to give him away free to a loving home. Was I still interested?

Good question. Christmas was over. Yet I still had that mental image of a dog running to Mark. "Yes, I'm still interested." We made arrangements to go see the dog down in Atherton; my sister Marguerite rode with me. The owners had two small children and another dog, so they'd decided one of the dogs had to go. He looked perfect. "My husband's out of town right now," I said. "Let me talk to him, and I'll get back to you with an answer in a couple of days."

I called Mark and told him, "I have a surprise gift for you."

"Oh?" he sounded noncommittal.

"It's what I really wanted to give you for Christmas, but it just didn't work out in time."

"What is it?" He didn't really sound curious.

"It's a dog—a Schnauzer."

He remained dead silent. I could tell he was shocked.

So I continued. "A male. He's eight years old, housebroken and very cute. And I'd like to get him for you if it's okay with you."

There was a long silence before I heard Mark's voice. "Why?"

"I know you've always wanted a dog, and I thought it would make you happy. And because I love you."

The rest of the phone call seemed a little tense. Mark had some of the same old criticisms of me, but he sounded more mellow even than he had at Christmas. It wasn't just my imagination. He wasn't ready to give me an answer about the dog, so I told him I'd give him a little time to think about it.

A couple of days later I made up my own mind and became the proud owner of one hairy gray bundle of energy named Daschell. Dasch for short.

Mark called a few days after that to talk about some details on our income tax form he wanted me to tell our accountant. "Go ahead and get that dog if you want," he said.

"I already did." And I told him all about how Dasch and I had been taking walks around the neighborhood and getting acquainted. We spent the rest of what turned out to be our best phone call yet, talking about Dasch. With Mark giving me detailed instructions on what to feed him, where and how often I should walk him, and how to groom Dasch.

The next time we talked I offered Mark a new argument in response to his past complaint that he didn't see any hope for our relationship. "If we believe God has the power to heal your body, then don't we have to believe he could also heal our marriage?" When Mark didn't argue the point, I hoped I was finally getting through.

All the emotional uncertainty with Mark was taking its toll at work. It seemed my heart wasn't in my teaching. I felt constantly on edge and rushed through things. I had difficulty going at my students' pace.

> But even as her impatience with Mark permeated all areas of Shireen's life, progress was being made. The two of them were talking regularly on the phone, about the dog, about business and income tax details, and about their relationship. On January 31 they talked for three hours. Much of the time Mark criticized Shireen and listed the barriers he saw to God healing their relationship. He complained that she never told him she needed him. (Though he'd criticized her in the past for not being independent enough.) He griped that one of the checks she'd stopped payment on was for a medical bill that now couldn't be included on their 1985 tax returns. (Though he'd been the one who withheld information on what bills needed to be paid.) He accused Shireen of never cutting the apron strings and truly leaving her parents to live with him. (Though he was the one living with his mother rather than his wife.) He quoted Scripture about the need for a wife to always obey her husband. (Though he chastised Shireen for "always preaching at me.") He also complained that all their planned remodeling work could have been done on their house if Shireen hadn't run him off. And he offered a long list of other "wrongs" that needed to be righted by Shireen if their marriage was to work.
>
> Shireen just listened and made notes. Some things she could change. Others she couldn't or wouldn't. But she didn't argue. At least they were beginning to communicate, really communicate again.

That night, at the end of five journal pages itemizing most of Mark's criticisms, Shireen wrote out a Bible verse—1 Peter 2:23— which says about Jesus: "When they hurled their insults at him, he did not retaliate; when he suffered, he made no threats. Instead, he entrusted himself to him who judges justly." And she meditated on that verse often in the following days.

About this time an older businessman-friend from church, Dick Horberg, called Mark during a trip up in Oregon. On his return to San Francisco, Dick reported that he'd had a nice conversation with Mark. "He said he loved you." I wanted to be encouraged by that; but I couldn't help wondering if Mark really meant it.

Sitting in church one Sunday during January, I opened the bulletin and saw a note to the congregation saying the deacons had voted to start a special "Perry Fund." Anyone who wanted to contribute financial assistance to the Perrys during their current medical crisis was encouraged to channel the money through this special deacon's fund. I was moved to tears right there in the service.

I had heard nothing of this plan ahead of time. But the help would be very welcome. Mark had begun chemotherapy under the care of his Oregon doctor and his twice-a-month, $250-a-shot treatments weren't covered by my medical insurance because Mark was out of state. I'd been sending Mark the money to cover the chemo each month, but my paycheck wasn't enough to keep paying it. Other bills were piling up.

So it was with real gratitude that I accepted the deacons' check at the end of the month. When I sent the money on to Mark, I told him the source, hoping it'd say to him what it said to me. That a lot of people really did care about him and about us.

Soon after the beginning of February, Mike Ryan decided to

visit Mark in Oregon. He hoped to get a more accurate picture of Mark's health and perhaps encourage him to come home, at least for a short visit.

The morning of February 11, Mike Ryan flew to Portland for the day. Mark and his mom met Mike at the airport and took him to breakfast. According to Mike, "Mark's defenses were up at the start. He quickly let me know he was never coming back to San Francisco. He said, 'People down there were killing me.' And he went on to complain about the lack of effective medical help he'd found in San Francisco, about the lack of acceptance from his friends, about Shireen's lack of support, about the stringent, restrictive diet he'd been on with Shireen, and about the way his creativity had shriveled and atrophied.

"I just let him talk," said Mike. "He told me, 'It's so much better for me up here. My family is here and they're more accepting and supportive than those in San Francisco. I'm eating anything I want to eat again. I've found a Christian doctor who listens to me and has me on a chemo routine that I can feel is helping. I feel as if I'm alive again.'

"He drove me around to show me his old stomping grounds, where he'd lived and where'd he co-owned a store. He showed me a garden love seat he'd constructed out of carefully bent green branches of an apple tree and declared, 'Even my creativity has begun to come back.' "

The more Mike and Mark talked, the more open Mark became. Mike shared the love and concern Mark's friends had for him. He talked about Shireen's love and commitment. And before he caught his afternoon flight back to San Francisco, Mike challenged Mark to at least come back to San Francisco for a visit. "He didn't make any promises," Mike said, "But the impression I got was that he'd at least give the idea some thought."

Mike's report encouraged me. Not only did he detect an open-ness to the idea of coming home, but Mark seemed to be in better health than I'd hoped. Mike said the lesions had shrunk with the chemo, and the swelling in Mark's leg had gone down. Mark continued to be convinced of God's healing, but Mark's mom told Mike the doctor felt Mark was in the advanced stages of KS and that he had a cough related to that which indicated infection in his lungs.

Mark surprised me with a late evening call on Valentine's Day. I filled him in on Ronah and Barry and little Braden; things were not looking good. Near the end of our conversation he said he'd been thinking about coming home for a visit before long. He didn't say when; but that didn't matter. I could hardly get to sleep that night—I was so excited.

A few days later, Mark gave me a date. He'd fly home for a week's visit on Saturday, March 8. My prayers were answered.

Or rather, that prayer was answered. Others weren't.

On Monday March 3 I went to a memorial service for the husband of one of my coworkers. On Wednesday that same week, I'd taken the day off work to stay home and clean house. There wasn't much to clean, but I thought I could at least have the bare floors mopped and freshly waxed for Mark's return. However, I didn't get to my cleaning; Barry called that morning to inform me that Braden had just died. So I spent the day over in Berkeley with my family.

On Thursday, Laurice Perry, a long-time friend of Mark's (from his days in the "lifestyle") who'd become a Christian and was now a dear friend of mine as well, volunteered to come over and help me with the housework. Soon after she arrived, I went to let Dasch out the back door into our fenced back yard. He'd just started down the long steps from the porch when I spotted a German shepherd waiting for him. And I saw a second German shepherd trying to get into the yard through a hole they'd broken in the fence.

I charged down the steps after Dasch to stop him. But the snarling German shepherd got to him first, and seized Dasch by the neck, shook him violently and flung him into the air. Blood flew everywhere. As I tried to snatch Dasch up from the ground where he landed, the big animal sank his teeth into my dog's backside and Dasch instinctively clamped his jaws onto my right wrist. I tried to pry his mouth open with my left hand as I ordered him to "Let go!" But when he did, I lost my grip and dropped him, which inspired the big dog to attack again.

Laurice stood up on the porch steps screaming, "Shireen! Get out of there!" The second German shepherd was in the yard now, circling warily. I reached for the garden hose lying on the ground near by, and when I yanked it toward me, the metal end whipped around and hit the first dog. He threw Dasch up in the air again and retreated. And as I screamed at them, both of the big dogs slunk off through the fence and were gone. Then, with my own blood streaming down my arm, I picked up the torn, bleeding body of my little Schnauzer to assess the damage.

Instead of mopping floors, Laurice chauffeured me across town to the vet, who insisted on keeping Dasch for observation overnight after she sewed him up. Then she drove me to the doctor to get a tetanus shot and have my own wound examined and bandaged.

Unable to drive or even write without pain, the floors didn't get done the next day either. It had been a terrible week. Mark was coming home tomorrow and I felt in no shape, either emotionally or physically, to give him a proper welcome.

Mark at work in the reception room of his office. Spring 1984.

Mark and Shireen's wedding day. September 1, 1984.

An oriental party hosted by Mark (front right) and Shireen (standing, second from left). Summer 1985.

Mark with Pastor Mike Ryan. November 1986.

Selecting a Christmas tree. November 30, 1986.

Mark still having fun a week before his death on February 28, 1987.

February 12, 1987.

CHAPTER NINE

I *WAS SO EXCITED TO SEE MARK WHEN* he walked off his plane Saturday afternoon that I didn't even mind that my enthusiastic greeting seemed quite a bit warmer than his. He was home. That was all that mattered. I wasn't about to be put off by a little coolness.

I hadn't known what Mark would feel up to doing when he came home. So I hadn't been sure what plans to make. Donna Ryan had suggested a coupon book. So I'd put together a booklet of fun, interesting ideas—one idea to a page. Some old familiar places we might go, some favorite things Mark had always enjoyed doing, and some new options I thought he might enjoy. For example: "This coupon entitles you to: A trip to Mt. Tam"; "A tour through the local Naugahyde Factory"; "An evening with friends"; "A walk along the pier"; "Explore favorite spots of Chinatown"; and more. I presented Mark with the coupon book and told him he could pick any of the options anytime he was home. Or he could suggest his own alternatives. I just wanted to do what he wanted to do while he was home.

The coupon-book idea worked on several levels. It helped smooth out some potential communication conflicts about expectations and what we would do when. It showed him I could take some initiative (something he'd complained about) and still allow him to take the lead in making the decision (another of his concerns). Plus I hoped the ideas I included would indicate that I could come up with creative things for us to do together.

Mark opted for one of the "dinners out" coupons. So we drove to Ten-ichi's, a Japanese restaurant that had long been one of our favorite spots. And after I filled him in on my dog-fight adventure, Mark talked easily about his plans for remodeling our house.

After dinner we took a short walk up and down Fillmore Street, stopping at one point and going into a dress shop to see the work of a contemporary Japanese designer Mark admired. While we were in that shop, the radio station being piped over the store's sound system played Amy Grant singing "El Shaddai," the song we'd had sung at our wedding.

Knowing how important symbolism was to Mark, I quickly looked over to see his reaction. There was none.

"Mark?" I finally asked as we walked out of the store. "Did you hear the song they were playing? . . . 'El Shaddai'?"

"Yeah." That was all he said. But I felt sure it had made him think. At least I saw it as a powerful confirmation—we were together again the way we belonged.

After finishing our walk, we drove back across town to Potrero Hill. And as we walked in the front door of our own home, Daschell came limping down the hall to greet us. It wasn't exactly the image I'd imagined of a dog bounding happily into Mark's arms; in fact, Dasch made a pretty pathetic picture with a big, plastic, cone-shaped collar around his neck to prevent him from turning his head and chewing his stitched-up wounds. But all that mattered was that Mark had finally come home.

Introductions were brief. "Mark, meet Dasch." The dog wagged his tail as best he could. And then Mark helped me give Dasch his medicine and clean his wounds with hydrogen peroxide.

Mark and I continued our conversation from dinner as he walked around the house and talked about where we'd put the new bathroom, what we'd do different in the kitchen, etc. When he referred to the bedroom as *my* room and the office as *his* room, I tried not to let it bother me. But it did.

I also tried not to let it bother me when he insisted on sleeping back in the guest room on the trundle bed instead of with me on the double-bed mattress I'd borrowed from my parents a few weeks before. If I could just be patient, I felt certain he'd begin to warm up. Lying alone in my own bed that night, I told myself, *At least he's home!*

Sunday morning at church a crowd of people swarmed around us to welcome Mark home with big hugs and concerned questions about how he was doing. And Mark responded warmly to our friends' concerns. Then we took a relaxing afternoon drive that made me feel as if we were courting again.

Eventually, I worked up the nerve to tell Mark how I was feeling about last night. "It bothered me to hear you refer to our bedroom as my room."

He said he was sorry ("But that's just the way I see it now"), and that he didn't feel it was "set in concrete." He said that right now it contained only my things, and he didn't think he'd be comfortable in there the way it was. He felt he needed his own space.

I let the issue drop and we talked of other things. Like his "explanation" of what had happened last September. He said he'd felt as if everything were building up around him, and he'd identified very much with the Old Testament prophet Elijah who had needed to get away from it all for a period of spiritual restoration and refreshment.

When I expressed surprise that he'd never shared these feelings or motivations with me back in September, he said he hadn't felt I would understand or accept his decision. So he hadn't felt free to talk to me.

I went to bed alone again that night. Before he'd come home, I'd told myself I shouldn't hold high expectations for this visit. That I should not push things, but just let Mark move at his own pace. That it would be enough just to have him home. But after a little more than twenty-four hours, I couldn't help feeling a little disconcerted by Mark's attitude toward privacy in the bathroom and his careful avoidance of seeing me, or letting me see him, in any state of undress. It made me feel as if we weren't even married.

I'd had a similar feeling on Saturday when I'd noticed that Mark wasn't wearing his wedding ring. But I waited for a couple of days before I asked him about that. He said he didn't know, he'd lost it somehow, somewhere, a few months before. He had no idea what had happened to the ring. When I thought about how angry he'd been with me for so long, I had to wonder if Mark had sometime thrown the ring away in a rage. But remembering some of the bizarre things he had done before he left back in September, it was easy to believe he'd done something bizarre with it and truly didn't know where it was.

We agreed I would go to work as usual every day that Mark was home, except for one. He needed his rest during the day, and the house would be quiet. Dasch stayed doped up with painkillers and antibiotics, so the two of them just lay around the house most of each day. In the evenings when I got home from work, they'd both be up for a short, slow walk. And we'd talk.

Whenever we reached an awkward place in our conversation, Dasch was there. We would talk to him or about him as we tried to care for him and monitor his recovery. Dasch was serving as an icebreaker, a tension reliever between us. As a neutral third party in the house, he demanded just enough attention to keep us from totally focusing on the delicate relationship we were carefully starting to rebuild.

Tuesday night Mark wanted to have dinner alone with his friend Bob Hartmann. So I went to a birthday party I'd been invited to. Wednesday evening we drove to Berkeley for a special homemade pasta dinner with Ronah and Barry. Mark was moved by Ronah's recounting of Braden's last moments—his labored breathing, his parents' fervent prayers and reluctance to give up, until Ronah finally realized she needed to let go. "I love you, Braden," she'd said. "You can go to Jesus now." Braden took one last peaceful breath and died.

We had an emotional but positive time with Ronah and Barry. Mark seemed warm, supportive and caring. My parents, Marguerite and Ed, and my brother Jay all stopped by Ronah and Barry's during the evening to greet Mark. While Mark acted cool toward them, his anger erupted as soon as we got in the car to drive home. He felt "ganged up on" by "everyone showing up uninvited" and intruding on our time at Ronah and Barry's.

I took Thursday off and we spent a fun, tension-free day driving around the city, visiting some of our favorite spots, exploring some interesting little shops and eating dinner at Mike and Donna Ryan's. As the week wore on, I detected a real warming trend in Mark, which freed me to be honest with him. I told him about the frustration and fear I'd felt back in September. He told me he'd felt I wasn't listening to him at the time and went on rationalizing his behavior for some time. I didn't argue. But I went on to talk about the sadness I'd felt at Thanksgiving and Christmas because we'd missed out on the chance to start the traditions we'd said we wanted to have. And I told him how much I'd been hurt by his verbal abuse and the harsh criticism that had dominated our communication for so many months.

Each day that week Mark seemed to soften a little more. And I felt more and more optimistic about the future of our relationship. I'd wake up early each morning and review the main principles in a book on marital communication Mike Ryan had recommended—just to remind myself of what I needed to be working on that day.

Friday night we cuddled on the makeshift mattress/couch and talked. Mark even said he'd like to come home again, but he didn't know when. And my hopes continued to climb.

Saturday was Braden's memorial service. But Ronah had told me early in the week she would understand if Mark wasn't physically or emotionally up to coming and that she felt I needed the time to be with Mark. Since I had done my grieving with my family the day Braden died, and Mark and I had already shared time together with Ronah and Barry on Wednesday night, the two of us spent a quiet, restful day together.

However, I couldn't shake the troubling awareness that Mark's visit was quickly drawing to a close. My jumble of feelings was so mixed. I wanted to feel glad that Mark expressed such confidence and felt so positive about the medical care he was getting in Portland; but I wished he felt he could find the same care in San Francisco. My spirits were buoyed by the obvious progress we'd made in our communication in just a week; but I realized that tomorrow he was leaving and we'd be limited to phone calls and letters again. His talk at the beginning of the week of coming home to stay was as much as I'd hoped for (and more); but now I wished he wouldn't go back to Oregon at all.

Saturday afternoon we went out to a movie and saw "Out of Africa." The film's powerful themes of romance, mortality, relationships and loss struck emotional chords deep within me. As we soberly discussed the movie over dinner, I realized Mark too had been touched by the story.

Perhaps it was the romantic mood created by the movie, the sad realization that Mark was leaving in the morning, the warmth and affection we'd shared the night before, or a combination of all those things. But when we got home, I decided the time had come for boldness. Leaving Mark sitting in the living room, I disappeared into the bedroom. Minutes later I returned wearing a red silk negligee Mark had given me the year before, and determinedly began to seduce my very surprised, but not-too-resistant husband. We held each other and enjoyed a sweet intimacy I thought we had both forgotten.

Finally, I invited Mark to come to bed with me. He smiled and shook his head. "I want to," he said, "but if I did, I don't think I'd get any sleep all night." I knew he had to get his rest; his return flight for Portland left early the next morning.

So even though I went to bed alone again on the last night of the visit, I felt a happy hopefulness that had been missing in my soul for what seemed like an eternity. Mark's feelings for me were still very much alive, and so was my dream that we would one day be together again as husband and wife.

Despite the optimism of Saturday night, or maybe because of it, driving Mark to the airport Sunday morning and watching him walk away from me down the jetway was one of the hardest things I've ever done in my life. I couldn't help thinking of Karen Blixen in "Out of Africa" watching the man she loved fly out of her life for the last time and then getting the terrible word that he'd died in a plane crash. And I felt this sudden gripping fear that I might never see Mark again. The thought seemed absolutely unbearable. I had to pray and ask the Lord to give me faith and love to replace the fear.

While Shireen knew what an encouragement Mark's visit had been to her, she could only hope it had affected him the same way. And it had.

His first day back in Portland he resumed his own journal writing for the first time since early September when he'd begun to get delusional, the week after he'd told the church about his AIDS. His entry for March 20 read: "Once again I try to write a journal after much delay. So much has happened. . . . My trip to San Francisco sparked my enthusiasm and purpose once again. Shireen and I made great headway in deepening our understanding and compassion for one another. Now I look forward to returning [home] . . . in God's time."

The warmth she and Mark shared the last couple of days of his visit freed Shireen to feel romantic for the first time in months. And she expressed her feelings in a letter she wrote Mark a few days after he'd gone back to Portland—a letter very different in word and spirit from any she'd sent to Portland before. She said: "Thank you, Mark, for the time of intimacy. I do miss the cuddles, your arms around me and our chats." And she went on to reminisce in writing about her most romantic memories with Mark: "The exhilaration I felt at our wedding when Mike introduced us as 'Mr. and Mrs. Mark Perry' for the first time." And that first night of their marriage—"What a special night you created for me with your tenderness and warmth. I will never forget it. Or our wonderful honeymoon."

The week in San Francisco continued to work its magic, and Portland began to pale in comparison. In the second entry of his new journal, Mark added, "How I long for the day to be in my own home again in San Francisco!"

And a little over a week after Mark's return to Oregon, I received a warm, loving letter, and the first long-distance communication since September that didn't include one negative comment or criticism of me. Mark expressed appreciation for my frankness and honesty and wrote, "I love you Shireen and appreciate your wonderful qualities that God has given you. And that makes you special to me. How I wish we were together right now; but I know the time will come."

But would it come soon enough? When Mark told me he'd just enrolled in a welding class at a local junior college so he could build topiary frames for creating plant designs, I lost some of my hopes that his return was imminent. He began talking about me making a trip up to Oregon for his sister's wedding celebration in June, but that seemed liked too long to wait. So I renewed my fervent prayers and recruited friends to pray with me that the Lord would somehow convince Mark to come home again before June.

The week after Mark had flown back north, I'd contacted our insurance company to report the loss of his wedding ring. The agent had filed the claim and given me the okay to replace the ring, as long as I covered the increase in the value of gold— which turned out to be only $35. So I'd gone to our jeweler over in Sausalito and had an identical wedding ring made. Whenever Mark did return, I wanted to have his ring ready as a welcome-home surprise.

Not that everything was now positive between us. One day in the first week of April when we talked on the phone, Mark seemed particularly discouraged. I worried about the cause of his depression and wondered if he was finally getting to the depression stage of the crisis cycle I'd been reading about—a cycle that begins with denial and progresses through anger, bargaining and depression to finally reach acceptance.

Perhaps the problem was more physical. Mark still didn't offer much information about his health. He acted touchy if I asked specific questions about his treatment—as if I were challenging him or doubting what he was saying. And he still spoke critically of my family—especially my parents—which troubled me. But I felt that something had been rekindled inside Mark, and we both seemed to be operating on the unstated, but underlying, assumption that we could put our marriage back together again.

Mark called the tenth of April with the word Shireen had longed to hear for so long. Mark was coming home the following week— with their household possessions.

When the happy phone call concluded, Shireen sat right down

and wrote Mark: "What joy! I'm ecstatic! How I look forward to you being home with me again!"

Up in Oregon, Mark began the strenuous, detailed work required to move. On the sixteenth he wrote in his journal: "Preparation to leave is taxing. I can't wait for the day . . . My energy level is low."

In San Francisco, Shireen anticipated the moment. Sunday the twentieth was the day. After church she stopped by the Ryans' house to get some encouragement from Donna. Then she hurried home to make sure everything was in order for Mark's return.

I threw on an old blouse Mark had never liked, to do the last-minute cleanup around the house. For his early-evening arrival, I planned to shower and dress in an outfit I knew he loved for me to wear.

As I pulled the vacuum out of the closet, the doorbell sounded. Walking down the hall to the front door, I could see a shadow of someone standing on the step. When I opened the door, there stood my beaming husband. I stood in the doorway, speechless with surprise, until Mark swept me into his arms and gave me a long passionate kiss.

"Mark!" I exclaimed when he let me catch my breath. "I didn't expect you for another few hours at least."

He grinned, "I couldn't wait. I woke up early this morning and couldn't sleep. So I got up and drove straight through."

"Thirteen hours?" *He has to be exhausted.* "You must have really wanted to get home."

"Yeah, I did!" he said as he kissed me passionately again. He obviously wasn't too exhausted. His excitement, so different from his cool arrival back in March, thrilled and nearly overwhelmed me.

Within minutes we were in our bedroom together and Mark noticed the small gift-wrapped box I'd placed on his pillow.

"What's this?" he wanted to know.

"It's for you, open it."

Carefully he loosened and slipped off the paper. He opened the box and lifted out the new wedding ring I'd bought him. He looked up at me and I grinned. As he slipped the ring on his finger, I realized there was nothing more symbolic or more significant I could have ever done to welcome him home. The emotion I read in his beautiful, brown eyes was all the thanks I'd have ever needed. But not all the thanks I got.

Mark took me in his arms and kissed me. And then we went right to bed. Unpacking the truck would wait till tomorrow. Mark was home! And we were husband and wife again.

CHAPTER TEN

*T*HERE WERE NO WORDS TO BEGIN TO express my happiness. But the next day I attempted to write a prayer of thanks to God: "Thank you, Lord, for bringing Mark home safely last night. What a joy to have him home! I praise you for the change you've brought about in his heart. What a treat to be able to play with each other, to get reacquainted with each other's bodies. Thank you for his asking my forgiveness for what he's done these past months. Thanks for his reassuring words of love and his tender kisses and hugs."

Mark had changed. I had changed. Living together again as husband and wife was like starting our marriage over again—a brand new beginning. And because I didn't know what further changes the coming months would bring, or even how many months we would have, I thanked God each morning for another day with Mark.

That togetherness was interrupted briefly a week after he came home when he flew back to Oregon to pick up his car and receive one more chemotherapy treatment. He was to be gone until the second week in May.

Though I knew for sure this time that Mark was coming back and when, those were two long, lonely weeks. The seven wonderful days we'd had made me anticipate his final, permanent return all the more. And the house, even filled again with our belongings, seemed particularly empty without Mark. Or even Dasch.

The day he'd flown back to Oregon, Mark had told me he'd gotten especially tired during the week because he hadn't been able to sleep during the day. Dasch's constant yapping at every sound he'd heard outside had made daytime naps virtually impossible. "I'm afraid," Mark told me, "either the dog has to go, or I do."

"You stay!" I quickly assured him. "The dog can go."

Dasch's previous owners had said I could bring him back if things didn't work out. So I called to say I'd be driving down the peninsula to Atherton to return Dasch. When Dasch and I pulled into the driveway of his old home, he happily greeted his old owners. But a few minutes later, when it was time for me to leave, he jumped into my car and growled when I reached to pull him out. Handing him over to his old owner and then driving away proved even harder than I'd imagined it would.

On the way home I pulled off the freeway at a scenic vista point, parked and sat in the car crying for fifteen minutes before I could see to drive home. I'd become very attached to Dasch in a very short time. Even though he'd not had time to become "Mark's dog" as I'd imagined when I first thought about giving Mark a Schnauzer for Christmas, I realized he'd served a vital purpose. Especially during that first, tentative, tension-filled visit of Mark's back in March. Dasch had played a valuable role in the restoration of our marriage, and I was going to miss his gray, furry face.

So in mid-May, when Mark returned to San Francisco from Oregon, driving his own car, the house was quiet. But we'd no sooner resumed the new life we'd begun in April, when I realized all was not well. While we'd both changed and he no longer attacked me with the same bitter intensity he'd used in those phone calls from Oregon, Mark still set a demanding standard for others; and he often criticized friends, my family and people at church (to me, not to their faces). When he got in one of his critical moods, it was as if anyone who disagreed with him, including me, was automatically wrong because he was always right.

This proud and critical spirit bothered me so much I began to pray about it. The very next Sunday I got an answer to that prayer when Mike Ryan preached a very clear and forceful sermon warning about the dangers of being a critical Christian and judging other people. One statement Mike made stuck in my mind as something I believed Mark needed to hear: "Blowing out someone else's candle will not make yours glow any brighter."

Mark also heard the message. In fact the sermon spoke so convincingly to him that Mark recorded a number of quotes from it in his own journal about needing to be more charitable and less critical of others. He also noted the statement: "Blowing out someone else's

candle will not make yours glow any brighter." And he determined
to be better about his critical attitude.

Mark tried to resume work on a new project with a favorite client,
but he quickly found he didn't have the energy. Just to keep up
enough strength to make it through each day, he needed morning
and afternoon naps. But his physical weakness didn't short-circuit
his creativity. He sketched quilt patterns and began talking about
teaming up with Shireen to teach a quilt-in-a-day workshop. The two
of them also planned and hosted a big congratulations party for
their friends Dave and Sissy Wells upon Dave's graduation from
podiatry school.

Decor for the "Foot Party" included numerous mannequin legs
(and feet) artistically placed around the house: sticking out of a
large urn, lying on the buffet as part of a flower arrangement, and
so on. The theme-related food included baked chicken legs, pickled
pigs' feet and biscuits Mark had shaped into tiny feet, complete with
little toes, and of course (toe) jam for the biscuits. Bad puns laced
the conversation throughout the party, inspiring far more groans
than chuckles. And the zany evening concluded with a dozen or so
friends, most clasping a mannequin foot, posing for a group picture.
Once again, after months of sadness and empty silence, the Perry
house was filled with the laughter of their friends.

A friend of Mark's named Elaine, who'd called to encourage him
many times while he'd been away in Oregon, invited Mark to
share the story of his experience with a number of people who
met regularly in a home Bible study. So, for the first time since
that Sunday back in September when he'd fainted in front of the
congregation of First Covenant Church, Mark went before a
group of people to talk about his AIDS and his faith in God. I
sat beside him and listened intently as he quietly, calmly told
about the events of the past fifteen months, since the day the

doctor had said he had six months to live. He talked about God's goodness and love, and he warmed my heart by mentioning "Shireen's wonderful support." Confidently, Mark said God was continuing to heal him through his ongoing program of chemotherapy.

Another important incident took place just a few weeks after Mark's return home. We drove with a group of church friends down to San José for an evening service of worship, praise and prayer at a charismatic church fellowship called the Vineyard. The service, which took place in a rented school building, began with almost forty-five minutes of worship and praise songs.

Then, right in the service, during a long period of silent prayer, several men, none of whom knew either Mark or me, gathered around us and began praying very specifically for Mark, his emotional and spiritual healing, and his relationship with God. I noticed tears rolling down Mark's face as these people prayed. After a few minutes, a woman standing directly behind my chair began to pray for me—for the healing of my anger, my feelings of betrayal, my tiredness and my relationship with Mark. Amazed that this woman I'd never seen before (and never saw again) could know my innermost feelings as if she were looking directly into my soul, I realized it could only be the Spirit of the Lord ministering through her to me. And I felt God's presence there in a powerful, uplifting way.

I also sensed something happened inside Mark. And between us as well. It was as if some huge barrier separating us shattered and fell. Though I wasn't to understand the depths of what had happened for some time yet.

> Mark hadn't been able to admit it to himself, let alone to anyone else, but much of the anger he'd been experiencing for months, the anger which had vented itself from Oregon in criticism of Shireen,

the church and friends in San Francisco was really anger toward God and toward himself. He was angry at God for allowing him to get AIDS and for not answering his prayers by healing the effects of the disease once and for all. And he was angry with himself for his own failures and the decisions of his past that had brought him to this point in his life.

But that night at the Vineyard Fellowship, Mark felt God's power and concern in a new way. In his journal he called it a "major turning point in the healing of my feelings toward God. Thank you, Lord, for renewed fellowship with you and the return of joy in our relationship."

That renewed relationship with God was further evidenced a few days later when he read and recorded in his journal two Bible verses that spoke to him, and which he thought should speak to anyone with AIDS. "Praise be to the God and Father of our Lord Jesus Christ, the Father of compassion and the God of all comfort, who comforts us in all our troubles, so that we can comfort those in any trouble with the comfort we ourselves have received from God" (2 Cor 1:3-4).

As the summer progressed, Mark had numerous chances to share the new comfort he was feeling from his revitalized relationship with God. He shared the story of his spiritual journey at a local meeting of Homosexuals Anonymous. He developed friendships with a couple other AIDS patients he heard about. And the two of us took part in a panel discussion at First Covenant—about AIDS and the workplace.

The church and our church friends continued to be a support to us both, in countless ways. In small ways, like Pat and Paul Gabriel's faithful delivery of a hot, homemade supper every Monday evening starting the week Mark returned from Oregon. And in big ways, like the continuing Deacon Fund gifts. Time after time, an unexpected expense would be followed by an unexpected check for almost the identical amount. During one particularly difficult month, we received a four-hundred-dollar medical bill and a four-hundred-dollar Deacon's Fund check in the same week. We became convinced both of God's provision and of the generous love of our church community.

The end of June, I took two weeks off so Mark and I could drive up to Oregon to his sister's wedding reception. On the way to see his family in Portland, Mark took me to Eugene to show me the university; where he'd lived during his college days; the store where he'd worked while he'd gone to school; and other places that had been important to him. As we drove, he shared memories with me, many of them for the first time.

During our week in Portland we also visited some friends whose little girl welcomed Mark with a bear hug around his knees that melted his heart and prompted him to share with me his longing to have children of his own. To be the kind of father he never had growing up.

Following the time with Mark's family, we got away by ourselves, just the two of us, for a few days at a friends' cabin at the ocean near Tillamook. We read, rested and took peaceful walks together along the foggy shore. After all the turmoil and pain of the preceding year, we rediscovered a depth of romance and intimacy that left both of us feeling absolutely euphoric and wishing we could freeze time forever. But we had to go back.

While on our vacation, in some of the Bible reading we did together, we read a passage that talked about "putting your house in order." Mark felt there was a clear message for him in that passage, a message he should take literally. So when we got back home, he began devoting much of his time and most of his physical energy to working on our house. I came home from

work one day during the summer to find the front hallway freshly painted. In early August he designed and built a scaffolding.
With his mom's and his brother's help, he sanded and caulked
the exterior of the house. After Mary and Bruce went back to
Oregon, Mark began to paint each day, for as many hours as
he could take being up out of bed and moving around.

It was also a Saturday in August when we held our "Quilt in
a Day" workshop for a half-dozen couples. We'd spent one Saturday beforehand creating our own quilt-in-a-day so we'd know
just what to expect. The long hours of creative teamwork required by that trial run proved to be an extremely insightful
experience for both of us. As usual, Mark wanted to take the
creative lead, but he also wanted me to take a vital role in carrying out the task. Because he had his usual hard time articu-
lating his expectations, I struggled to know what he wanted and
he'd get frustrated, feeling I wasn't trusting his intuition and
artistic instincts, if I asked for clarification. It was a perfect mi-
crocosm of the basic communication problem in our marriage
relationship. But because we both were determined to do this
workshop together, we were able to talk through the troubles
and share insights into what was happening and why in our
communication. In the process our understanding reached a
new, exciting level.

Not that everything about our relationship was now smooth
sailing. It wasn't. Mark still sometimes felt I wasn't responsive to
his feelings or expressive of mine. And I felt he sometimes
lapsed into his critical mode, always feeling he had to be right
when we disagreed and that I was always wrong. But in praying
for and about Mark and asking God to take away his pride, I had
a clear insight; I realized that when he was demanding and
critical it was because he didn't feel worthy of love. So I began

an even more deliberate campaign to affirm Mark, to tell him every day how much I loved him and how special he was to me.

That campaign, and Shireen's prayers, paid off almost immediately. One day at the end of August, Mark wrote in his journal these words: "Remorse. Toward Shireen for not accepting her love. Not feeling loveable. Forgive me, Lord Jesus. [My] pride has to go."

And the day after their second anniversary he wrote, "Shireen and I had a relaxing weekend. But the [urge] to sleep was incredible. I slept most of Sunday and rested during the picnic on Mt. Tam.

"What a treasure Shireen is to me and how she puts up with my demands, my whims. How blessed I am with such a wife. Thank you, Lord."

That was about the time I came home one evening to find Mark lying on the daybed. In giving him a hello hug, I sensed something was wrong. And he immediately began telling me about a program he'd been watching on a local Christian television station. "They interviewed a lobbyist on the program who was urging viewers to support a law that would require the quarantining of all AIDS patients!" (The LaRouche Party had succeeded in getting such a proposition on the California ballot for the upcoming elections that fall.) "I'm so upset seeing that kind of attitude on a Christian TV program. There was no Christian compassion, no compassion at all. I'm so angry, I'm going to write a letter," Mark declared. He had a pad of paper beside him and had already jotted down a few notes.

"You know what else we need to do, Mark," I said. "We need to pray that someone with a different attitude, a different perspective, will be able to go on that show and help viewers understand the other side of AIDS."

"You're right," Mark agreed. So we stopped and prayed right then, never imagining how that prayer would be answered more than six months later.

Mark's cough, which he'd had for some time, began to get worse. His doctor referred him to a specialist, and he went in for chest x-rays on September ninth. On the tenth Mark called me at work with the disheartening news. "Shireen," he said, "the doctor called and said she wanted me to go to the hospital today. She looked at the x-rays, and she thinks I may have pneumocystis." (*Pneumocystis carinii pneumonia* is one of the most common opportunistic diseases to strike AIDS patients and the most acutely life-threatening one.)

I could hear the discouragement in Mark's voice. "I'll be home as quickly as I can get there," I told him. And the moment I hung up, I began to pray: "Okay, Lord, you're really going to have to help us this time!"

I truly believed he would.

CHAPTER ELEVEN

MARK TOLD THE DOCTOR HE NEEDED
another day.

He and a couple of friends had just knocked out the entire
back wall of our dining room and reframed it. The only barrier
between inside and outdoors was a sheet of plastic covering the
gaping hole where we planned to install a set of solid oak
French doors we'd found in an antique store on our Oregon
trip. So Mark called the friends back and late that night they
finished hanging the doors and installing the oak paneling on
the dining room wall. The following day, September 11, knowing the house would be safe, Mark checked into St. Mary's
Hospital.

His specialist assured Mark that if everything went well, she'd keep him in the hospital only ten to fourteen days. I visited him every day and called him often from work.

One of his first nights in the hospital, I walked into his room and gave him a big kiss. "Shireen," he said excitedly, "I want to show you what the Lord revealed to me today." And he got out his Bible, read a passage from Psalms that had triggered his insight and went on to say how he'd come to see how much affirmation he needed and how it was a serious ego problem that made him so critical of others and always needing to be right when he and I disagreed.

I listened to him admit to these problems, which I felt were really the root of all the communication problems I'd been praying about for months, but hadn't wanted to raise for fear of starting an argument. And I realized God was continuing to work in Mark's life, in his own timing. *Thank you, Lord,* I prayed.

Unfortunately, Mark's physical healing wasn't going so well. To treat the more immediate threat of the pneumonia, the doctor had to suspend Mark's chemo for the KS and pump him full of Septra, a powerful antibiotic which caused, as side-effects, constant itching all over the body, depression, and violent, continuous nausea. His cough worsened at first and only slowly improved. But even then, Mark suffered constant nausea, his KS lesions worsened again, he experienced pain through his whole body, and he grew alarmingly weak.

One night I sat beside his bed, holding his hand and watching his familiar sleeping face. Each breath had to be fortified with extra oxygen pumped into him through small plastic tubes looped over his ears, along his cheeks and inserted into his nostrils. He opened his eyes and whispered, "Shireen. I feel as if I'm going to die. I'm so tired and there's so much pain."

I squeezed his hand. "You're gonna make it through this, Mark," I told him. "Just hang in there. And in a few more days you'll be going back home."

Another night I was sitting beside his bed, offering all the words of encouragement I could, when Mark asked, "Shireen, do you think you could get in this bed beside me?"

"I don't know," I grinned. "Let's see." I lowered the side rail, Mark scrunched over to the far edge of the bed and I slipped in beside him. For the first couple minutes I wondered what a nurse would think if one of them walked in the room to find us cuddling together in that narrow hospital bed. But lying there, holding my sick husband in my arms, I soon forgot all about the nurses. For a few minutes it felt as if we were alone in the universe and everything was warm and well with the world.

Mike Ryan visited Mark in the hospital regularly. My brother-in-law Barry came across the bay to see him. Mark's own brother John drove up from Fresno. And a small prayer group of church friends came to encourage him. Michelle, who was a member of the group, brought her guitar. And as they sang praise songs with Mark right in his hospital room, his spirits rose.

Mark's physical condition did eventually begin to improve. The doctor finally let him come home on the ninth day, hoping that the return home would give him an emotional lift that would carry over to his physical recovery. But his legs and lungs were now so weak he barely made it back up the long steps to our front door. And the unrelenting nausea and pain made him miserable.

On Sunday afternoon, a day after he had come home from the hospital, I walked into the bedroom where he lay resting and talking on the phone with Laurice, who'd called to check on him. As he told Laurice how discouraged and frustrated he felt, he wept. So I sat beside him on the bed, just to be with him and offer any comfort my presence might bring.

When he finished talking and hung up the phone, I held him and told him I could see how discouraged he was. His passion for life was gone. I assured him that it would be okay to express his anger, depression and pain to God. And as we talked, I began to pray, just as if I were including God in our conversation. "Lord, you know how discouraged Mark is right now. Please give him some point of encouragement right now. Take away his nausea and pain."

Mark followed my lead and began sharing his deepest feelings out loud—as if God were there in the room with us. He told God: "I'm discouraged, Lord. I'm angry about what's happening to me and I'm in so much pain. I can't stand this any longer. Please do something to lift this from me, or just take me home, God."

I held Mark for a while in silence. And then I left him in the room to rest. An hour or so later he came out of the bedroom almost ecstatic. His depression had lifted.

For Mark, and for me, the answer to our prayers was convincing evidence that God still cared. That he was with us, and he'd continue to be with us, whatever lay ahead. Mark got so excited about his dramatic improvement that he couldn't even sleep that night. And by the next Saturday, Mark felt strong enough to go with me to a wedding for a colleague's daughter.

Not that Mark appeared suddenly, completely healed. The lesions remained, along with an occasional cough—both constant reminders that the AIDS still resided in his body. His toe stayed swollen and sore. And his candida yeast infection continued without relief. (Candida is a white bacterial yeast ordinarily kept under control by the body's immune system. But it goes out of control in many AIDS patients, growing under the fingernails and toenails and often lining the mouth and esophagus with a thin, white coating. Mark regularly sucked medicated lozenges to combat the candida in his throat.) Still, he felt better than he had in the hospital undergoing his pneumonia treatment.

Mark had been so heartened by the friends who came to pray and sing with him in the hospital, that as soon as he got back on his feet again, we began going once a week to Michelle's home, where the group gathered to pray and sing. The love and support Mark felt from the friends in that group restocked his own spiritual reserves, and the chance to shoulder and pray for the concerns of others gave him a chance to reach out and be a help to someone else. The result was that Friday nights became a highlight of Mark's weeks. And the catalyst for a new burst of creativity.

I rolled over in bed about three o'clock early one October morning to see the bedside light on and Mark propped up on his elbows, scribbling something on a note pad. And humming to himself.

"What are you doing, Mark?" I mumbled.

"Listen to this, Shireen," he said, obviously wide awake and excited. "It's a song the Lord has given me!" And he began to sing words to a tune I'd never heard before. "What do you think?" he wanted to know when he finished.

"That's great," I responded. And I meant it. But I guess Mark realized he wasn't to get meaningful music criticism from me at that hour of the night.

"Go back to sleep," he told me. "I'll let you hear all of it in the morning."

He was still excited when I awakened the next morning. And he sang me the song he'd written in the middle of the night— a song of praise to God. He called it "Jesus Our King":

We lift up our hands, O Lord, to you.
We lift up our hearts, O Lord, to you.
We shout hallelujah, Jesus our King.
Hallelujah our King!

As we trust and abide, O Lord, in you
Fill us with love, O Lord, for you.
We shout hallelujah, Jesus our King!
Hallelujah our King!

We open our lives, O Lord, to you,
For guidance and life, O Lord, from you,
We shout hallelujah, Jesus our King!
Hallelujah our King!

Over the next few weeks, Mark Perry's creativity found outlet in a number of songs he wrote—some scrawled out by the glow of a bedside reading light in the middle of the night, others written in the sunshine. But taken together they provide a picture-window view into the innermost recesses of Mark's soul.

In the midst of his own weariness and pain, he wrote a song called "His Rest" for his friend Sean, who also had AIDS. Then he drove to the hospital down in San Jose where he sang these words for Sean:

May I hug you, my hurting friend,
And sit with you and cry.

Let us pray to Abba Father
and humbly ask him why.

Let me comfort you, my friend,
Share your burden and your woe . . .

Blessings to you my friend,
He will carry you through.
Enter his peace
And his rest.

In the midst of his own emotional struggle with the uncertainties
of his future, Mark penned a song called "Hope." And the man
Shireen's family had nicknamed Mark the Spark also wrote a song
he called "The Spark of Jesus."

But despite his expressions of hope, Mark continued to struggle.
Physically, his symptoms slowly worsened. Emotionally, his sweet
days and times of encouragement with Shireen and his friends in
the prayer and praise group were counterbalanced by long hours
of loneliness and discouragement. Spiritually, he tried to reconcile
his love for and faith in an all-powerful God he believed had the
power to heal him, with the mounting evidence that healing wasn't
happening.

One particularly low day in early November, Mark talked about
how tired he was. "I think I'd rather die and go to be with God
right now," he said. "There just doesn't seem to be any purpose
in living."

But the very next day, while I was at work, Mark received a
phone call saying the Christian Broadcasting Network (CBN)
was looking for a Christian with AIDS to interview for an end-
of-the-year news special they were putting together. They'd

heard about Mark's story and wanted to know if they could send a crew out to San Francisco to interview the two of us. Mark told them yes. When he told me after I got home that night, I immediately flashed back to a news feature on AIDS I'd seen on TV only a couple weeks before. As the reporter had interviewed a mother whose young hemophiliac child had AIDS, I'd been thinking to myself, *I don't know if I could be as vulnerable about my private life as these people are.* Now Mark had committed us to doing the same thing.

I might have protested. But seeing the excitement on Mark's face, I realized he had found a purpose in life again. And I knew we were to do it.

The week of our scheduled CBN interview, Mark went to the doctor for another checkup. When I came home from work that evening, he broke the bad news. The doctor had told him lesions were starting to break out up and down the inside of his throat. And from his cough, and listening to his chest, she thought the pneumocystis had come back.

Mark said he'd told her he didn't want to go back in the hospital for another round of pneumonia treatments. She'd understood. "You just want to be comfortable then?" she'd asked. When Mark had answered "yes," she'd nodded her acceptance of his decision and suggested a local hospice program. "It's staffed by trained medical professionals who provide basic care and assistance for AIDS patients in their own homes."

Remembering Mark's misery with the pneumocystis treatments back in September, I also understood Mark's determination not to go into the hospital again. I told him I wanted to support him in whatever decision he made. And he decided to contact the hospice for information.

After his checkup, before he told Shireen that evening, Mark had gone to see Mike Ryan for a long emotional talk that covered, among other things, the subjects of healing and God's sovereignty. Either during that conversation, or in reflecting on it afterwards, Mark came to a new plateau of peace and acceptance of whatever lay ahead for him. He verbalized it a few days later in front of the CBN cameras when he said:

"Yes, there's a sense of feeling cheated. . . . I have a beautiful relationship with Shireen, and now it looks to be cut short. . . .

"If it's his plan to wholly and completely heal me, I accept it. But the franticness is gone. If it's his will for me to die tomorrow, I'm ready for it. As the apostle Paul wrote, 'To live is Christ, and to die is gain.' And I feel that in my heart."

All in all, the CBN film crew spent the better part of three and a half days with Mark and Shireen. At home. Over at Shireen's parents' for dinner and a time of singing praise songs. On a walk around Stowe Lake in Golden Gate Park. At church on Sunday morning. And Mark walking and talking alone with the interviewer on Castro Street, in the heart of San Francisco's gay community, on Saturday night.

The long grueling hours in front of the cameras exhausted Mark and Shireen both. But it also gave them the opportunity and the framework to think back and talk about every aspect of their four-year relationship. In the process, they verbally and publicly expressed their mutual appreciation, love and commitment to each other—knowing the words were true, camera or no cameras. And when the film crew finally packed up and left late Sunday afternoon, Mark and Shireen went out to the House of Pancakes and ordered breakfast to celebrate their survival.

A week after the CBN interview, on the thirtieth of November, a friend of mine volunteered to drive us down to Half-Moon Bay to buy a Christmas tree. And the next day, while I was gone to work, Mark decorated our tree with an "old-fashioned Christmas toy" theme. Later that same week, we went over to Oakland and helped trim my parents' tree. And the two of us worked together with friends to decorate the interior of the church for Advent. Like two little kids, we loved and anticipated the tradition, excitement and fun of the Christmas season, which was Mark's favorite time of year.

Mark had resumed chemo treatments every two weeks when he went off the pneumonia medicine the first of November. And a hospice nurse had begun coming by the house once a week since the end of November just to check Mark's vital signs, evaluate any changes in the disease, answer questions and suggest changes in medication or care that might ease Mark's discomfort. But even without any formal medical training, I was sure Mark's health was in a gradual, but steady decline.

We slept in late on Saturday morning, December 13. When I finally roused, Mark said he wanted to stay in bed and sleep some more. So I got up alone. A little while later, as I puttered around the kitchen, the realization seemed to slip up on me: *There may be more and more days like this when Mark doesn't feel up to getting out of bed. There may even be a day before long when Mark won't even be here with you.* Those weren't welcome thoughts; so I quickly forced them to the back of my mind. But not for long.

By noon it was clear that Mark felt wretched. Part of the problem was the chemo treatment he'd had the day before. But he also seemed to be coming down with a flu bug. Whatever the primary cause, Mark decided there was no way he could go to his friend David Wallin's wedding that afternoon. Knowing that David had been Mark's first Bible study leader and had once been an important person in Mark's life, I knew Mark had to feel terribly sick.

I went to the wedding by myself and sat with Donna Ryan. I cried (and Donna cried with me) through the entire ceremony, realizing that I'd probably be doing more and more special things by myself, without Mark beside me to share the big or even little experiences of life. What a terrible feeling!

When I got home, Mark was lying on the daybed in the front room, watching TV. He asked how the wedding went and I began to cry. When I gained enough control to get the words out, I told him about the feelings I'd had at the wedding. How the reality had hit me. How sad it made me to think about him not being with me. How much I was going to miss him.

Then we cried together as he talked of his own sadness and grief. And he admitted he didn't want to leave me behind either.

Later that evening, Mark wrote this prayer:

"This chemo is the worst ever. Help me to get through it, Lord, one more time. How wonderful it is this holiday to be with my wife, family and friends. Thank you for making it possible.

"Another turning point today with Shireen and me. Facing our grief with our emotions, confiding in each other. We've both been weeping today.

"Bless my loving wife, my best friend and lover. Thank you, Lord, for answering my dreams by bringing Shireen into my life. Thank you for showing me and demonstrating the love you have for me— through her. How I thank you for her love. For your plans for our lives are perfect. You know our deepest needs and desires and mine are to be loved."

Though God didn't seem to restore Mark's physical body to complete health, he did bring deep emotional healing. We had seen a miracle take place in our marriage. So even as we faced what seemed to be Mark's imminent death, we knew our relationship had been completely, wonderfully healed.

CHAPTER TWELVE

*T*WO DAYS LATER, STILL RECOVERING from the effects of his last chemo treatment combined with a flu bug, Mark made a long list in his journal—a list of creative projects he wanted to tackle. First on the list was "a handmade book to give Shireen for Valentine's Day" that would include his songs, selections from his sketch book over the past two years, poems, and "perhaps some dried flowers." He wanted to make shadowbox frames to display his arrowhead collection and a collection of hand-tied fishing flies he'd gotten from his stepfather.

He sketched out ideas for making a Christmas chest out of an old chest he and Shireen had—painting it with gold paint, adding decorative handles, a new lining and Christmas designs. Another idea:

"Make kimono using antique silk obie. Line with applique design to hang in bedroom." He proposed making a cabinet in the bottom of an old pendulum clock to hold and display a collection of small clay curios Shireen owned. And his last recorded idea was: "Make front room into creative project room for inviting people over to work together."

No matter how low Mark got, his creative mind never quit.

Mark felt strong enough again by Christmas Eve that he and I and his sister Barbara, who'd come to stay with us over Christmas, went to my parents' house for my family's big traditional Christmas Eve dinner. When we returned home late in the evening, we had our small private Christmas around our own tree.

We'd agreed ahead of time that we'd have a small, inexpensive Christmas by making presents for each other. So I presented him with a shirt I'd secretly made for him during my lunch hours at OCB. And he gave me a beautiful set of pillowcases with an old-fashioned butterfly pattern he'd cross-stitched for me using striking contemporary colors of thread.

As I *ooh*ed and *ahh*ed over his creative handwork, he presented me with another present. Then another and another. Each time I'd exclaim over a gift, he grinned and handed me another box. Somehow he'd found the time and energy to sneak out shopping to select a variety of beautiful things: a sixty-inch costume pearl necklace; a gold watch; an oblong, jewel-colored, plaid scarf; an iridescent paperweight; and a set of gold earrings in an abstract, curled design.

I'd never in my life gotten so many special Christmas presents from one person. I felt overwhelmed with Mark's loving thoughtfulness. But watching Mark sitting there, relishing every minute of my surprise and joy, I couldn't help contrasting the happiness I felt at that moment with the pain and loneliness I'd experienced the Christmas before. I realized Mark was trying to make it up to me this year.

Christmas afternoon and evening, dozens of friends and family members honored us with their presence in our own home for our annual, traditional Perry Christmas Open House. Mark and I each had a warm, wonderful evening talking with people—many of whom we hadn't seen for months and some of whom Mark didn't expect to ever see again. We both went to bed exhausted. But lying there, side by side with Mark, I wholeheartedly agreed with his assessment: "This has to be the best Christmas ever."

At the same time, I couldn't help wondering what next Christmas would be like. If I would be having another Christmas with Mark.

Much of the remainder of our holiday time centered around our families. Mark's mom and two aunts came for a visit. And on New Year's Eve Marguerite hosted a fancy, black-tie party to celebrate both the New Year and my brother-in-law Ed's birthday. Mark didn't have the energy to be out long, so we went to the party late, arriving around eleven o'clock and staying just long enough to help usher in the new year. When we got home, he hardly seemed to have enough energy to get out of his tux. So I had the intimate pleasure of helping him undress for a change. And then we enjoyed a warm romantic time together.

The pain medications Mark had been on—Darvoset, then Darvon—took a little edge off his pain for short periods of time. But the nausea and depression had remained constant for some time.

However, the third of January was Mark's best day in weeks. Neither of us could understand why he felt so encouraged and energetic. Until the next day when we began to hear from friends who told us our CBN story had been on the air on the third as part of CBN's "700 Club" program. Tens of thousands of viewers had joined in prayer for us, and Mark had felt the results. It inspired him to make a long list of ideas in his journal, practical things that concerned people could do to show love and compassion to AIDS patients. (See Appendix A.)

But as the holiday season passed and I went back to work, Mark again faced an uncertain future of long, lonely, increasingly painful days. Feeling particularly discouraged on January 6, he and Mike Ryan spent a long time praying together for some sort of breakthrough, some sign from God that would encourage Mark that he had more yet to live for. That same afternoon, CBN called to say they'd received such positive feedback on the short feature they'd done about us that they wanted the two of us, along with Mike Ryan, to fly to the 700 Club's Virginia studios the first week of February to appear with Surgeon General C. Everett Koop for a live discussion of AIDS and the Christian community.

That same day, we had an oxygen tank delivered for Mark to use when he felt the need. After trying it for a while, he said he'd forgotten how good it felt to breathe deeply.

Mark's spirit's soared. Once again he felt God had answered his prayers by easing his discomfort and giving him something to anticipate. And he was further heartened in the days and weeks that followed with a steady stream of letters from people who'd seen us interviewed on CBN and were writing to say they were praying for us.

Perhaps even more heartening was something that happened when we were visiting Barry and Ronah one evening. The doorbell rang. Barry opened the door and in traipsed the Longacres, a family from Ronah and Barry's church—mother, father and four children, ranging from nine years old down to about eighteen months. They'd heard we were going to be in Berkeley that night, and the children had come to deliver something special to Mark.

All the children at Ronah and Barry's church had been praying for Mark ever since we'd publicly announced his AIDS. And the Longacre children, whose parents told us they prayed for "Mark and Shireen" every night in their bedtime prayers, were there to present Mark with a box of cards several of the church kids had made for him.

The children acted shy and uncertain. But Mark tried to set them at ease by shaking each child's hand, asking their names and thanking each one personally.

These kids had decorated the outside of the box and written this message: "We have made a box of cheerful messages. Pull one out each day to know we are thinking of you." Mark was deeply touched. And even more so as he opened and read some of the cards.

One little girl had made a flower using a drinking straw and cutting the petals out of construction paper. Attached to her flower was a note which said, "God gives clothes to the flowers. He will also care for you and Shireen."

A four-year-old boy had pasted a paper face on a straw and dictated this message which his teacher wrote and taped on his creation: "This is a puppet. If you ever want to play, he is yours."

There was a little picture of a girl with a large red object in her hand which said, "A little girl with an apple; don't let your heart be troubled."

Another picture of apples said, "God gives us apples from the kitchen, and love from him." And a cutout valentine face declared, "We all love you and remember to pray for you every day." And a five-year-old girl who'd taken blue foil paper, glued on a couple of strips of colored paper and added a few abstract dots and lines, explained: "This is a scared bug because he didn't think anyone was there. But God was there."

Those cards meant so much to Mark. He put the box on a bookshelf in our front room and each day took out a different card and placed it on top of the box as an inspirational reminder of those children's love. And God's.

Mark needed all the encouragement he could get because his physical condition began steadily deteriorating. His legs and feet had been swollen for some time. The edema had begun to worsen and spread to his arms. None of his pants and only a few of his shirts fit comfortably. The lesions in his throat and on his larynx made swallowing painful and distorted his voice. He coughed more, and his lungs began to fill with fluid.

He made the decision to begin a daily, two-week-long regimen of radiation therapy for the lesions on his legs. But the sessions drained him. Every evening I'd rub lotion on his legs to ease burning and itching the radiation caused. But I had to rub gently, or the skin would peel off in layers.

But where Mark had always been so private about his medical treatments in the past, I noticed he seemed anxious to tell me all about the radiation sessions at the hospital. And about what he and Maria, the hospice nurse, discussed about his medication and care.

This new openness about what was happening medically, what he was experiencing and feeling physically, gave me the feeling that the final barrier between us had been knocked down. Any last little remnant of distrust was gone, and we could talk about anything.

It seemed as if our communication had finally reached the

point I'd always dreamed about. Sometimes we'd look at each other and know what the other was thinking. I could anticipate a need without him even voicing it. We seemed to be perfectly tuned into each other's emotional and mental frequencies.

And it wasn't just my imagination. Two different people at two different times said the same thing to me: "It's as if you two had been married for thirty years, you communicate so easily with each other." After all our struggles to communicate, this finally felt like victory.

Mark psyched himself up to be cheerful every night when Shireen walked into the house after work. Evenings were his best time. He'd almost always be up for visitors who came. And when he and Shireen were alone together, they talked or read aloud. Sometimes they'd read books about marriage, family or communication and discuss the implications for their own relationship. Other times they just read imaginative stories such as C. S. Lewis's *The Lion, the Witch and the Wardrobe.*

But the long, daytime hours when Shireen worked and Mark was alone with his escalating pain quickly devoured his emotional reserves. He hid his depression for a while before the hospice nurse picked up on it and asked Mark about it. When he finally conceded and began taking an antidepressant, his moods began to level out. Yet still the pain increased. Mark and the hospice nurse discussed the alternatives. Mark told Shireen the decision was to begin morphine. And they scheduled a special conference for January 22 to talk about it with those closest to Mark.

We invited my parents and siblings, Mike and Donna Ryan, Michelle and a handful of other friends from church. About twenty people crowded into our living and dining room, taking up all the chairs and spilling onto the floor.

Mark introduced Maria, his nurse, and Lorna, the hospice

social worker. Then Maria told us: "Based on our experience with AIDS patients, and judging by Mark's condition right now, it's our best guess that he has perhaps two months to live." She went on to explain that Mark had been suffering constant, severe pain and depression for some time, and the pain was drastically increasing. She said Mark had been taking an antidepressant for a short time already and now she and Mark had decided the time had come for him to begin taking morphine to control his pain.

The nurse hastened to explain that they'd begin with the smallest possible effective dose; that the idea was to give Mark only as much narcotic as he needed to endure the pain and yet stay alert enough to interact with the people around him. She talked a little about the myths and the misgivings some people have about morphine. And she went on to describe the effects we might see in Mark.

Mark also shared some, talking about his recent battle with depression, and letting people know he'd welcome phone calls during the day when he tended to be at his emotional low point. (Up to this time, close friends and family had avoided daytime calls, thinking Mark's greatest need was rest.) Then Mark and the nurse answered any questions (there were just a few) anyone had about his current condition and treatment.

After that the hospice people slipped out, and Mark invited everyone else to stay for ice cream and cake in honor of my thirty-third birthday, the very next day.

The next night Mark and I had our private birthday celebration when he took me out to Ten-ichi's for a Japanese dinner. The day after that, a Saturday, we drove our two cars through the rain, over to Walnut Creek to have routine tune-ups. While the cars were being worked on, we visited some old friends of mine Mark hadn't known very well, and we both had a great time. But when we returned home that afternoon, Mark told me, "I don't think I should be driving anymore. I just don't feel safe on the road."

With his weakness, he didn't feel confident in his ability to respond quickly enough if something happened. And he didn't want to risk the safety of anyone else.

I knew giving up driving was hard for Mark. It further limited his independence and his mobility. And it increased his isolation from the outside world at the very time when loneliness had become one of Mark's biggest battles.

But two days later, when I came home from work Monday night, Mark said he wanted to rearrange the living room—something we'd used to do once a month or so. Suddenly he was taking initiative and seemed like his old self again. He even talked about other changes we could make in the future—such as moving the living room furniture into the front room and having a bigger dining room for entertaining.

I felt so encouraged to see him animated and optimistic again. He seemed to be gaining strength.

Mark hadn't felt up to going to the Friday night prayer and praise group for a number of weeks. So when Michelle had heard Mark and the hospice nurse talking about his battle with depression, she decided to bring the gang to Mark. As many as a dozen members in the group who worked flex-time jobs or were their own bosses began bringing lunch to the Perry's home two or three days a week to eat with Mark and spend a few minutes praying and singing with him.

One particularly memorable day, the group used their lunch time as a chance to throw a little surprise birthday party for Doug, a new Christian who'd grown up as a Jehovah's Witness and had never ever had a birthday party before. And Mark was so thrilled to be part of Doug's historic event that he went on and on about the details when Shireen got home that evening.

Other friends and family members would phone Mark to talk. And Shireen made it a point to call from work two or three times each day just to encourage him and hear how he was doing. The result of all this attention was that Mark's feelings of loneliness and the worst of his depression lifted.

Friday the thirtieth of January, Shireen's dad drove Mark to the hospital for his last scheduled radiation therapy. Back at home after the appointment, Mark had to be helped by Jack Irvine up the long steps to the front door. Mark had to pause several times to catch his breath. When they finally made it into the house and Mark sank, exhausted, onto the couch, he said to his father-in-law, "I think that's probably the last time I'll ever come up those steps."

After work that Friday afternoon, I hurried right to my parents' house. The plan had been for Dad to bring Mark back to Oakland after his radiation therapy; we were all going out to a new Cajun restaurant to celebrate Marguerite's birthday.

Dad was home. But Mark hadn't come with him. When Dad related what Mark had said about the stairs, and told me Mark had wanted me to go on to dinner without him, I rushed to the phone and called Mark to say I'd rather come home and be with him. He told me not to do that; he was weak and just needed rest. And he insisted I stay for the party and represent us both. Convinced he'd feel worse if I missed the family festivities, I reluctantly agreed to stay.

But I spent most of the party thinking about Mark. It was awful to realize what Mark had told Dad might be true, that he indeed might never climb the steps to our house again. Even as I sat there in the middle of my loving, supportive family, I realized there was going to be a huge, gaping, black hole in my heart when he was gone. And no one else would ever fill that place.

At some point during the evening I realized I'd withdrawn into my own private thoughts; I'd not truly been participating in the laughter or even the conversation going on around me all evening. I'd detached myself and become a silent observer, a pattern that had once been a habit of mine when I felt reserved, insecure or shy in a group—even in my own family. It was a pattern I'd somehow broken since Mark came into my life. There was something about his presence that drew me out. Or maybe it was the sense of his support that gave me the confidence to stretch, to risk opening up in a group.

That was just one of the areas in which Mark had enabled me to grow. Being married to Mark Perry had made me a better person; he drew out many parts of me I hadn't even known were there. He called me his "flower," and he truly helped me blossom as a person.

What happens when Mark dies? I'll lose my greatest inspiration for growing and stretching as a person. An even more troubling thought: *Maybe I'll lose all the growth I've made in the past four years. Maybe I'll revert to the old Shireen.* I didn't want that. But because Mark was such a big part of the growing, changing person I'd been and enjoyed being, I suddenly feared that his death would mean the death of the best part of me as well.

I wept as I tried to explain these terrifying thoughts to Mark when I got home. "Don't you see," I cried. "You've helped me to grow so much. Without you I'm afraid I'll slip back. I need you so much."

He told me he knew I'd be fine. That he saw real strength in me. And he comforted me by putting his arms around me and holding me tight as I cried.

But even that encouragement reminded me how much I needed him. And how much I was going to miss him.

CHAPTER THIRTEEN

*N*OTHING SEEMED TO SLOW MARK'S physical decline.

Weakened now to the point that he took oxygen much of the day, it looked impossible for Mark to fly cross-country for the "700 Club" interview. I didn't understand it; the invitation had been such an encouraging answer to prayer. Now we were going to have to cancel.

But when we called CBN the week before the broadcast date to say Mark just wasn't going to be able to make the trip to Virginia, the producers said they wanted to go ahead with the show anyway. They'd fly Mike Ryan east as planned, to be in the studio with Surgeon General Koop; and they'd do a remote interview with Mark and me from our own home.

The CBN camera crew arrived on the Perry doorstep about four o'clock on the morning of February 4 to set up their equipment. Mark and Shireen dressed and took their places on the living room couch. Back in the Virginia studio, the "700 Club" ran some of the CBN footage of Mark and Shireen shot back in November. So when the show shifted live via satellite to Mark and Shireen in San Francisco, the deterioration in Mark's condition seemed almost startling. He'd been so healthy back in November—by comparison. Now he sat in front of the camera with dark purple spots on his face, oxygen tubes running into his nostrils, his voice weak and strained through the lesions in his throat. The edema was spreading so quickly that even Mike Ryan, sitting in the studio in Virginia and watching Mark and Shireen's interview on the monitor, noted how much more swelling there was in Mark's hands since he'd seen him just the day before.

Asked during the interview by Ben Kinchlow how he felt about the seeming likelihood that God wasn't healing him, that he was indeed going to die, Mark nodded and smiled. "I believe he can [heal me]. But God has the master plan for my life. I can't see the master plan. But he does. And I have to trust Him. If he heals me, fine. If not, I know [my death] is part of a bigger picture."

Mark's death now seemed inevitable and imminent—to Shireen and Mark both. Mike Ryan took Shireen to a mortuary to learn about the options. Mark decided the cost of transporting his body to Oregon to be buried in a plot he'd bought up there was unnecessary, so Shireen and Marguerite went to a local cemetery to arrange for a plot. Mark participated in every decision, even making notes about what he wanted to happen at his own memorial service—right down to the songs he wanted sung.

February 11 turned out to be a very special day for Mark when his friend Wilburn Duncan flew in from Arizona for the day just to visit Mark. "Duncan," as Mark always called him, had been a Christian businessman who'd helped Mark get started in business up in Oregon. He'd been like a father-figure to Mark, believing in him and encouraging him to use his skills. He and his wife had also been sending us money from time to time to help out in our financial crisis, so we knew and appreciated their care. And we had a wonderful time together that day as Duncan and Mark talked and laughed and prayed together, knowing it might be the last time they'd see each other.

On the evening of February 11, Laurice came for supper with us. Afterwards, she sat at the foot of our bed while I massaged Mark's painfully swollen legs and feet (as I'd done almost every night since he'd returned from Oregon). Out of the blue, right there in front of Laurice, Mark asked me, "Shireen, do you think you'd ever get married again if I die?"

Yet Mark didn't catch me cold. The question had popped into my own mind just the day before as I drove home from work. And my first reaction, sitting there behind the wheel, was *No way. Mark could never be replaced. I can't imagine ever having another relationship like I've had with Mark.* But then I'd realized I couldn't just discount God's will. If the time came when I felt God was leading me to marry again, I'd want to do it. And I could see that the need for companionship might be a strong reason.

Those had been my thoughts the day before. So that's what I told Mark.

His face remained sober and thoughtful for a moment. Then he looked up at me with a mischievous, sheepish kind of grin and said, "I'm jealous. Give me a kiss." I leaned up and our lips met for a moment before he leaned back and smiled. I knew he understood, and it was okay.

On Thursday February 13, while Shireen was at work during the day, Ronah and Barry and Marguerite and Ed came over to the city to visit Mark. They knew Mark's energy level was low, so they tried to keep the conversation low-key and relaxed. But Mark kept querying Ronah and Barry about the remodeling they were doing at their house. "Have you ordered your light fixtures yet?" he wanted to know. "What have you considered?"

"Have you decided on window treatments? Maybe I can help." Warming to the task, Mark sent Ronah into his office and told her right where to look on the shelf for his lighting and window treatment books. When she brought them back, Mark went through them, poring over pictures and enthusiastically discussing a variety of options. Ronah and Barry eventually spotted some vertical blinds they really liked; Mark made a note and promised to order the blinds for them from one of his suppliers.

But the shot of adrenalin he seemed to get from sharing his professional expertise soon wore off. The morphine kicked in, and he became so groggy that he apologized to his in-laws for his drowsiness before they left.

Late the next evening, Mark's temperature began to climb—100°, 101°, 102°, 103°, 104° and still rising. Somewhere around 105 degrees, Mark slipped into unconsciousness.

Lucy Ogden, an emergency room nurse who was a friend from church, stayed with me through the night. Together we bathed Mark's legs and arms with cold towels and alcohol to try to bring his temperature down. When that failed, Lucy suggested we call Maria, the hospice nurse.

Maria arrived within minutes, and when Lucy left for an all-night drugstore to buy Tylenol in suppository form, the two of us stripped Mark completely and tried the cold-water-and-alcohol-bath routine over his entire body. At one point, as she leaned over the bed close to Mark, Maria softly whispered, "You can let go now if you want to, Mark. You don't need to keep fighting."

But I wasn't quite willing to give up yet. "I think he still wants to live," I told her. "He's not ready to go yet. There are plans he has, things he wants to do this next week."

Indeed, Mark didn't let go that night. He kept fighting. About two o'clock on the morning of February 14, his fever broke. As it dropped, he came out of his coma. By afternoon he was feeling strong enough that he asked me to get out our card box where we kept a selection of cards for all occasions. When I set the box beside him on the bed, he ran his finger along the alphabetized dividers until he came to *V.* He reached in and pulled out a handful of Valentine cards. When he found the one he wanted, he presented it to me. And after I'd read the loving, romantic sentiment, he handed me the leftover cards saying, "You can file these back under *V.*"

As I did, he reached over and picked up a Kleenex tissue lying on the bed and handed that to me also, saying, "Here, file this under *K.*" And we both succumbed to a fit of laughter. Despite his weakness, Mark's playful humor was alive and well.

But Mark's voice remained weak, sometimes hardly more than a whisper. When I'd bend close to try to hear him, he'd lean up and surprise me with a kiss. Each time he caught me with an ambush kiss (and it happened a lot those days), Mark would grin at me. And his eyes would sparkle the way they always did when he was happy or excited.

Around Saturday noon, Michelle called from Southern California on behalf of several members of the prayer and praise group who'd been down at Anaheim that week for a Christian conference. I reported that Mark had almost failed to make it through the previous night, and that he seemed stronger now. But even as I was on the phone with Michelle, Lucy called out that Mark's kidneys had begun to fail and she was having trouble getting a good pulse. I quickly got off the phone, but before I did, Michelle promised the group would be praying as they headed home, and when they reached San Francisco later in the evening they'd come straight to the house to see Mark—if he was up for company.

When they called again later to check on Mark, he was doing better and said he'd like company. So they arrived at our house about nine-thirty that evening. And the entire group, complete with guitars, crammed into the bedroom around Mark's bed and rejoiced that Mark was still alive and they could all be together again.

Propped up in bed, still far too weak to get up, but dressed for company in his gray Japanese happy coat with red Japanese lettering, Mark lifted his hands and sang song after song with his friends, including the song he'd written in the middle of the night four months before:

> We lift up our hands, O Lord, to you.
> We lift up our hearts, O Lord, to you.
> We shout Hallelujah, Jesus our King
> Hallelujah our King!
>
> As we trust and abide, O Lord, in you.
> Fill us with love, O Lord, for You.
> We shout Hallelujah, Jesus our King,
> Hallelujah our King!

"It was such an awesome, inspiring sight that none of us will ever forget it," said one of the people who was there that night. "Mark looked at the verge of death, but his face glowed with happiness as he raised his hands and sang to the Lord."

Before long, Mark felt such a surge of energy that he asked to get out of bed and came out in his wheelchair to the living room to sit and talk for a while with Shireen's father. After a few minutes, he went back to bed, greatly heartened by his surprising level of strength.

Sunday Mark's kidneys began to malfunction again; he quickly bloated worse than ever with the toxic fluids backing up inside his body. I called the prayer group and asked them to pray specifically for Mark's kidneys. They did, and having heard how low Mark had been in the early hours of Saturday morning, the group and other friends from church organized a prayer chain and gave me a list of who would be praying at what hour of the night, so I could feel free to call anytime there was a new concern or change.

By Monday morning Mark's kidney's had begun functioning once more. As he was able to finally urinate, the edema immediately began to subside until you could actually see his kneecaps and his anklebones again.

Mark had been getting up and shuffling around the house a little, using a cane the previous week. Now we got him a wheelchair so he could still get up when he wanted to; but he usually only lasted a half hour or so at a time. From this point he was pretty much restricted to bed—which meant he was propped with pillows in a semi-sitting position to enable him to breath. His oxygen remained on twenty-four hours a day, and he needed almost constant care to administer his regular medication, clean and dress a huge, open bedsore on his tailbone, care for his bodily needs and keep a more regular check on his vital signs.

Since the hospice group just didn't have enough staff to be with Mark around the clock, Lucy Ogden organized a team of volunteers from the church who would fill in the gaps and provide Mark with constant companionship and care while I was gone to work. They also helped do the routine household work so I could spend as much time as possible with him. Lucy herself moved into our guest room and stayed every night, setting her alarm so she could check on Mark and give him his medicine every three hours.

All we could do was try to keep Mark as comfortable as possible, pray and let him know people still cared about him. On the hospice nurse's recommendation, we began to restrict Mark's phone calls and visitors. I'd screen his calls or let him know when someone asked if they could visit him and always let him decide what and who he felt up to. He received bundles of cards and letters—over two hundred just from people who'd seen us on CBN—and not a day would go by without some family member or one of the core members of the prayer group calling us or stopping by.

Often he'd request that Michelle or another of the prayer group's musicians play and sing for him—sometimes beside his bed, other times a little farther away out in the living room. We had praise or relaxing music—either live or recorded—going twenty-four hours a day—which was one reason visitors often commented on how peaceful the house seemed when they walked in off the busy city streets.

Shireen continued to work most days those weeks—usually going in late or coming home a little early. She and Mark had agreed she would maintain as normal a schedule as possible. But her life for those weeks was far from normal.

Lucy Ogden, who was with Shireen more than anyone else in

those final days of Mark's battle, described what she saw between Shireen and Mark: "They went through a stage of love most couples never experience. They got a real understanding of what happens when love is stretched to the breaking point.

"In Shireen I witnessed the epitome of tenderness and patience. A total giving of herself as she focused entirely on the needs of Mark, her best friend and lover.

"And when he looked at her, his eyes were saying 'There's my love.' She was his joy, his comfort, his support, his love. When she was home, he always wanted her close by.

"When I'd slip into their bedroom in the middle of the night to check on Mark, I'd sometimes just stop at the foot of their bed and watch Shireen snuggled up next to Mark, asleep. It reminded me of Christ's promise: 'I'll never leave you or forsake you.' "

But the effort to keep Mark going was taking its toll on Shireen.

I was so tired. Physically and emotionally. I dragged myself out of bed on the morning of February 26 to get ready to go to work. In the shower I cried and prayed, "Lord, this can't go on much longer. Either heal Mark or take him now!" Feeling guilty about that sentiment, I hastened to add that my first choice was healing.

That evening, Sue Hawthorne, a member of the prayer and praise group, picked up Joe Fleming, another group member at San Francisco International Airport, and drove him to the Perry house to see Mark. Joe, a pilot with American Airlines, gave Mark his hat to wear, and the two of them joked around for a while in the bedroom. After a time, when the two men were alone, their talk turned serious and Joe confided in Mark that he thought he was falling in love with Sue. Mark asked him if he'd shared his feelings with Sue, and Joe admitted he hadn't. So Mark, who must have learned something from his own experience with Shireen, told Joe, "You really need to share your feelings with her." (On Mark's advice, Joe soon did just that later that same night. And a little more than a year later, Joe and Sue were married.)

Friday afternoon, when I walked into the bedroom wearing a crisp white cotton blouse with a pink ribbon bow tied around my neck, a gray and pink paisley pinwale corduroy skirt and matching pink shoes, Mark smiled and commented on how beautiful I looked.

"Thank you," I said. "I dressed just for you."

My response seemed to move him almost to tears. So I took his hand and sat beside him on the bed for a time to talk affectionately together.

Friday night Mike and Donna Ryan came for a visit. At one point Mike helped me prop Mark into a more upright sitting position; Mark's bloated upper body now weighed so much I couldn't manage him myself. "I guess that's okay," I said, when we got him situated. "Are you sitting on your donut, Mark?" (He had a foam pillow with the center cut out to keep from rubbing his bedsore.)

"Shireen," he replied. "Don't be so serious. Yes, I'm on my donut—my disco donut." And he launched into a little routine doing disco motions with his arms and singing about his "disco donut." His silly antics looked so funny, all four of us cracked up.

All day Friday, Mark had seemed to be slipping. He stopped urinating again, and the nurse upped his morphine dosage a bit to counter the increased pain from the fluid in his lungs. The periodic entries on his medical chart that day made note of "increased edema . . . crackling and labored breathing" and a "nonproductive cough."

His breathing became more labored as the evening went on. So Ronah and Marguerite, who'd come over to San Francisco to visit, decided to stay the night to be with Shireen. Since they hadn't come prepared to stay over, Shireen went to her closet and pulled out a selection of her nicest lingerie. A fire-engine red outfit for Marguerite. A silky blue one for Ronah. And one of Mark's favorites for herself.

Lucy Ogden had gone back to her guest bedroom to get ready for bed about the time Shireen's sisters decided to stay. As she tells it, "I came out of the bedroom a few minutes later to find all three sisters dolled up in these gorgeous, sexy outfits. And there I stood in my flannel PJs."

Lucy shook her head and said, "Will the real night nurse please stand up?" And all four women collapsed into laughter.

Lucy went in to check on Mark a little later. As she leaned over him, he lifted his heavy, swollen arms up around her and pulled her down on the bed beside him to whisper, "God bless you, Lucy, for being here for me and for Shireen. I really love you, and I really appreciate it." With tears in her eyes, Lucy hugged him back.

At 1 A.M. when she checked on Mark, his every breath seemed a major effort, and Lucy heard gurgling in his chest. That condition continued through the night, as Shireen sat beside him, holding his cold hand. At six the next morning Mark wouldn't respond enough to sip juice from a straw, but he did take a little with his morphine from a medicine dropper. However, swallowing triggered coughing.

At about nine-thirty in the morning, he slipped into a coma. Lucy stepped out of the bedroom to tell Ronah she didn't think it would be long now. So Ronah began trying to call relatives.

I sat beside Mark on the bed, holding and massaging his hand as I talked to him. I kept saying "I love you, Mark." But he didn't respond. "If you can hear me, squeeze my hand." Still no response.

Jerry Huckabee, one of Mark's closest friends from church

and the prayer group, was in the room with me. "If you can hear us, Mark, raise your right eyebrow," he said. Mark's eyebrow moved, ever so slightly.

"He can hear us, Shireen," Jerry assured me.

So I kept holding his hand and saying over and over, "I love you, Mark." After a while, feeling I wanted to be more creative in my expression of love, I got out a Bible and began to read Mark the beautiful poetic expressions of love from the Song of Solomon. Still no response.

Throughout the morning, his breathing slowed. And his color worsened.

At 1:05 P.M. Jerry sat at the foot of the bed praying. My sisters sat waiting in the living room. I stood by Lucy, watching Mark breathe as she checked Mark's pulse. And he took his last breath.

Lucy knew. "He's gone, Shireen." I thought *No! He's going to take another breath. Any second now.* But he didn't.

I sat on the bed beside Mark for a while with my head on his shoulder, crying and praying he'd come back. Praying that God would work a mighty miracle and bring him back whole again. But he was finally gone. And there's no way to adequately describe the feeling, the mixture of grief, of not wanting to let go, the relief that his pain was over and he was finally with the Lord whom he dearly loved, the feeling of void in my life—not so much pain as an aching hole, a hollow emptiness, in my very being.

Ronah began trying to phone relatives. And she immediately called the prayer and praise group, several of whom had gathered that morning at Joe Fleming's to pray for Mark. They arrived within minutes and were soon followed by my parents and a number of other friends.

Everyone gathered around the bed, and we began singing some of the praise songs Mark had written, singing as if we were lifting his soul to the Lord. As we sang, I cried and stroked his head, thinking, *This is the last time I'll ever be able to run my fingers through his hair.*

By the time the weekend hospice nurse arrived a short time later, the house was crowded with friends and family. And as he sat in the living room, asking questions he needed to ask to fill out his required paperwork, the nurse looked around at all the people and said, "Mark was fortunate to have so many people who loved and supported him. I've had two other AIDS patients die this weekend. The only people with them were their attendants. They died alone."

Mark Perry died just as he'd lived his last days . . . surrounded and cared for by a multitude of people who loved him. He was not alone.

CHAPTER FOURTEEN

*T*HE NEXT COUPLE OF DAYS WERE AN emotional blur of decisions and arrangements. But my family and friends surrounded me with support.

On Monday I went to the flower market to buy a huge array of cherry blossoms, and ended up with a gift of pink and white blossoms from one of Mark's friends, a flower merchant. And I borrowed Mark's favorite giant vase from Bob Hartmann along with a pink floodlight and created what I called "The Mark Perry Floral Arrangement" at the church. Mark had requested donations to AIDS ministries in lieu of flowers, so my special floral tribute was to provide most of the decor for Mark's memorial service. And on Monday night, Mike Ryan and I planned the details of the memorial service in accord with the wishes Mark had shared with us over his last few weeks of life.

Tuesday evening, in the final minutes before the service, I walked into the narthex of the church to see people filing into the sanctuary. And the thought struck me, *What would Mark be doing in this situation?* I knew immediately: he'd be greeting the people, welcoming them and trying to set them at ease.

So that's what I did. Until the service began, I did what Mark would have done. I mingled and stood at the door, smiling, shaking hands with some, hugging others, and thanking everyone on behalf of Mark and me for coming. As I did, I felt a warm sense of satisfaction knowing Mark would have been pleased.

> The service began with Sue Hawthorne leading the congregation in a half dozen or so praise songs. Then Mike Ryan prayed, "Heavenly Father, we are here this evening to offer you a celebration of praise for the life of Mark Perry. We are grateful for the miracle of his life and the privilege that it is to have known him."
>
> At the conclusion of the prayer, Mike told the hundreds of people gathered in the sanctuary of First Covenant Church: "What you've just participated in is a little of Mark Perry's life over the past months. The songs we have sung have been the songs of worship which have comforted him in his pain."
>
> Then Mike introduced the CBN tape of Mark's testimony which Mark had asked to be played, "so he can once again speak to us. Let's listen and let God's spirit comfort us through Mark's own words."

And there was Mark. Alive on the screen. His voice amplified through the sanctuary, saying, "My name is Mark Perry. Six years ago I was saved by the blood of the Lord Jesus Christ. And I walked out of homosexuality. Two years ago I was married, and six months later I had to tell my wife I had AIDS. . . ."

He was talking about his experience and his dissatisfaction with the gay lifestyle, saying, "I kept wanting more. I wasn't getting whatever it was I was searching for—which was really love. . . . I got fed up thinking, 'There has to be more than this continuous cycle of people in my life.' " And he talked about the change that eventually took place: "As I began to read my Bible, I wanted to read more . . . I found my identity. I found out who I was, who I was meant to be as a man."

The narrator was discussing how Mark's story of healing from homosexuality challenges the assumptions of the gay community, and he went on to say that "it raises even more serious issues with the church." And then there were a series of exchanges between the interviewer, Mike and Mark:

Mike   If I have a righteous indignation, it is with the attitude of a lot of men in ministry across our country. I run into pastors, particularly outside of San Francisco, who have absolutely no use for the gay community. Now that kind of attitude obviously doesn't honor the Lord, because the Lord loves and died for every member of the gay community. And we have to love the sinner, while helping him deal with his sins. If we would just be honest with ourselves and stand up and look in the mirror to see the sins we have in our own lives that the Lord's been merciful enough to forgive, we have no business saying God can't forgive or that he doesn't want to forgive members of the gay community.

Narrator   What do you think the effect of this crisis is going to be on the church?

Mike   Well, a lot of our sons and daughters are going to come down with AIDS.

Mark   It's frightening to think . . . we're just on the horizon of seeing a real epidemic. And there will be very many needy,

needy people. The church should be preparing now for these needs. And that is just not happening.

As the tape continued, Mark admitted his feelings about his diagnosis: "Why me, Lord? What is going on? You delivered me from [homosexuality]. Now it's with anger, much anger, a sense of feeling cheated for the beautiful relationship that he's given to me and now it looks cut short. It's a very hard thing, even now, to deal with. . . . Shireen's my best friend, and I love her dearly."

But he went on to say: "If it's his plan to wholly and completely heal me, I accept it. But the franticness is gone. If it's his will for me to die tomorrow, I'm ready for that. And I'd welcome it. The apostle Paul said, 'For me to live is Christ, to die is gain.' And I feel that in my heart."

The tape concluded with Mark reading from 1 Corinthians 15:52, 54, 55: "The dead will be raised imperishable, and we will be changed. . . . Then the saying that is written will come true: 'Death has been swallowed up in victory. Where, O death, is your victory? Where, O death, is your sting?' "

Interspersed with the congregation's singing of a number of the songs Mark himself had written were opportunities for Mark's friends to offer words of eulogy.

The Perrys' neighbor, David Smith-Walsh, expressed his appreciation for Mark's influence which led him and his wife, Amy, to become Christians. Laurice testified to the change that had taken place in Mark's life since she'd first known and partied with him in the bars on Castro Street, and how it was the change in Mark's life that caught her attention and brought her to Christ.

Lucy Ogden talked about Mark's peace and love for others in the midst of the suffering she witnessed in caring for him those last nights. Michelle Fontaine told how Mark had modeled Christ in his life. Shireen's brother-in-law Barry cited a line of dialog from the movie *The Color Purple*—"It really makes God mad when people go through the fields and don't see the color purple"—and he said, "Mark helped me to see the color purple. . . . He helped me to appreciate God's creation in a deeper way."

Pat Gabriel told about visiting Mark the Wednesday night before he died. As she walked into the bedroom where he was lying, he told her, "I need a hug." Seeing how sick and fragile he looked, she leaned over and gave him a small, careful hug. But that wasn't enough for Mark. "No!" he'd told her, "I want a BIG hug." So she'd hugged him again.

Donna Ryan shared about the time she told Mark how hard it was to watch him suffer. And he'd responded, "There's been more joy in my life this past year than in my entire life."

In the lonely weeks following Mark's death, I took comfort in the words these friends and others shared that evening in his memorial service. I also found comfort in what I was able to share during the service: "Despite our short marriage, it was full. And I think the Lord allowed us to live out and to fulfill the verses that we had chosen for our marriage and our life together. I want to share them with you, because they meant a lot to Mark. Hebrews 10:23-24: 'Let us hold fast the confession of our hope without wavering, for He who promised is faithful. And let us consider how to stimulate one another to love and good deeds.' "

In the days and weeks after his death, I came to a deeper understanding of how much Mark had stimulated me, how much he'd meant in my life. And just how much I'd lost.

On March 7 I wrote in my journal: "Immanuel means 'God with us.' What a comfort! Father, thank you. You are with me in my grief, my loneliness and my fears. My biggest fear is forgetting—the feelings of the precious times with Mark.

"Realizing that three and a half years of him in my life was so brief. Yet we were so united and close at the end, again experiencing an almost perfect marriage. To then have it broken again, this time by you, Father . . ."

Two weeks later, on March 21, I wrote: "Thanks for the reminder that you are my friend, that I can share intimate moments with you. It's difficult for me to realize this because there's a need for someone tangible.

"You taught us so much about intimacy through each other, for each other, and for you. You know how much I miss Mark and long to be held and have him talk to me, encourage me, keep me balanced. I guess I'm having to learn a new perspective on your love for me, Lord."

About that same time I commented to a friend, "It seems life will never be normal again." Her response was, "You're working out a new normality, Shireen."

She's right. That's what I've been doing ever since Mark's death. And in the process I've done much reflecting on our experience.

Sometimes when I hear about some new development in AIDS research or read about someone who's still living five years after the diagnosis, the *why?* questions creep back into my mind. I don't suppose I'll have all the answers I want until I get to heaven with Mark and ask the Lord myself.

I do believe what my father told me after he learned Mark had AIDS. He said, "Shireen, I know it was God who brought you and Mark together." I don't understand it all, but I believe God sees the master plan, and I trust him more now than ever, because he showed himself to Mark and to me. He answered so many prayers. And we felt his presence and his peace so convincingly in the months before Mark's death that I could never again doubt his caring for me. He taught us both so much through our experience.

Mark and I learned about tears and about grieving. We learned about communication and commitment. But most of all, we learned the meaning of love.

And in the time since he died, I've had a number of opportunities to share some of those lessons we learned together. Just a month after his death I received an invitation to appear, along with Mike Ryan, on the very same Christian TV show which had upset Mark a few months before when one of the guests had advocated quarantining AIDS patients. I'd never imagined that when we'd prayed that God would send someone else to that show to offer a more compassionate perspective on the AIDS crisis, that I would be that person. But that's what I did as I told our story and shared the loving, supportive response of our church friends.

I still miss Mark. I miss his supportive arms around me and his encouraging words when I come home frustrated by something or someone at work. I miss the gentle smile and the sparkle in his eye. I miss his excitement and enthusiasm for the big and little things in life. I miss the accountability for growth and the vulnerability and closeness of our relationship. I often long for the warmth of his touch. His tenderness. I miss his stimulating creativity, his fresh perspective on my everyday problems and the world around me. I miss his spiritual encouragement and his affirmation of me as a woman. But I've tried to take to heart what I said at the memorial service: "There is sadness . . . but also joy. There are times when each of us will be lonely for him. And that's okay. We can cry on each others' shoulders for a time. Then we can rejoice that Mark is with his Heavenly Father, in his Heavenly Father's love."

Mark knew he was loved.

Indeed, Mark Perry died having found, and knowing well, the love he'd searched for much of his life. He found it first, along with a new identity as a person, in the acceptance and love of God's son, Jesus Christ. Then he found it in the acceptance and steadfast love of a woman who clung fast to her wedding vows, and to him, in the midst of a storm that battered them both for two years. And finally, Mark found love in the caring support and affirmation of his church and his friends who surrounded and embraced him (both literally and figuratively) during his difficult last days on earth.

In a very real way, Mark's life and his death put him in the middle of two communities at war with each other—the gay community and the Christian community. And Mark Perry's story stands as an invitation to both communities to take a good hard look at him, and at themselves.

To the gay community, his story promises hope—hope for finding that love which so many thousands, like Mark, are looking for. To those feeling trapped in their homosexual lifestyle, Mark's story promises hope for change. And to those thousands of others with AIDS, Mark's story promises the hope of God's comfort and strength and peace in the midst of their suffering.

To the Christian community, Mark and Shireen's story—their testimony to God's grace, their life and love together, and the compassionate model of their church and Christian friends—presents a different message.

To the Christian community, this story is a reminder of facts many in the church would rather ignore: More than fifteen thousand people died of AIDS before Mark did. Thousands have died since. And even the most conservative estimates now predict tens of thousands more will die of AIDS before the end of this century.

To the Christian community, Mark and Shireen Perry's story has a final message. Asked at the end of their last CBN interview what they thought AIDS patients and their loved ones wanted from the people around them, Shireen said, "I think we want people, especially people in the church, just to have Christ's love and compassion rather than condemnation and judgment."

Appendix 1
What's Your Response to AIDS? A Case Study

The following is based on actual families Shireen knows. She's used this case study to foster discussion in a workshop she's done titled: "Touching the Untouchable." We included it here to help you think through your own response to people with AIDS. It could serve as the basis for discussion among co-workers, in families, or with church groups searching for a Christian response to people with AIDS.

Case Study: The Johnson Family
Meet the Johnson family: father, Dan; mother, Judy; and 8-year-old daughter, Sandy. Only a handful of people know Dan has AIDS. He suffers from cancer (Kaposi's sarcoma) and periodic skin infections. Because he has reached the stage where he tires easily and is sick often, Dan has just recently turned in his resignation at his office. Yet there are good days when he feels able to do things. Some days are particularly difficult emotionally and mentally for Dan.

Judy must work, especially since Dan is not working. Sandy knows her father is sick with cancer, but she does not know he has AIDS. Dan and Judy wonder how they should tell Sandy her father has AIDS. Or should they tell her at all?

Judy struggles to find the time and energy to devote to her work, her husband, her child and the household on days Dan is unable to do much around the house. Neither Dan nor Judy want him to go into the hospital. But there is no hospice organization in their community. They try to find and coordinate for themselves the resources they need. But they have little energy for the task. And the costs of the basic services they require seem insurmountable when they're already financially strapped.

Both Dan and Judy feel Sandy's needs are being neglected as a result of their situation.

What can you do for such a family?

Looking for Perspective
Ask:
1. What are the different needs here? Try to identify the individual needs first (Dan's? Judy's? Sandy's?), then the needs of Dan and Judy together, as a married couple and as parents. Consider also the needs of all three together as a family unit.

2. What is the biblical (Christ's) attitude we ought to have? What response would be biblical? Shireen has noted the following passages as pertinent to this two-part question: Mark 1:40-42; Luke 5:12-14; Matthew 8:1-4; 1 John 4:16-21; 2 Timothy 1:7-10, 13-14; Matthew 25:31-46; Matthew 7:1-12; John 11:17-37; Romans 12:9-21.

3. What practical steps could you take to help meet the needs of this family? For ideas to add to your own, see appendices 2 and 3.

The response needed in cases of AIDS is similar to that needed by cancer patients. But often the fear of AIDS is more contagious than the disease.

Appendix 2
What You Can Do to Help People with AIDS:
Mark's Suggestions

One day, the month before he died, Mark Perry made a long list of small, thoughtful ways anyone could help an AIDS patient or his family. Then he, Shireen and their friend Lucy Ogden (who now heads up a ministry to people with AIDS and their families in San Francisco) brainstormed some additions to his list.

If you've ever wondered how you could be a friend and help a person with AIDS or an AIDS patient's family, here are a few suggestions from Mark. These lists are by no means exhaustive; perhaps these ideas may prompt you to add some of your own.

Practical Help
1. Prepare and deliver a dinner for the patient and/or family.

_____ Once   _____ Once in a while   _____ Once a week

2. Do grocery shopping.
3. Drive patient to doctor's appointment.
4. Read a good book onto a tape and leave it for the person to listen to at his or her convenience.
5. Pick up prescriptions.
6. Do load(s) of laundry.
7. Help with housecleaning.
8. Tackle a fix-it job that's going undone around the house.

9. Deliver packages or mail to and from the post office or UPS.
10. Provide some financial assistance.
11. Find or offer housing for out-of-state family and visitors.
12. Check on and inform family of community resources.
13. Adopt a child for the day, if children are involved.
14. Other _____
15. Other _____

Be a Friend
1. Play games like checkers, chess, etc.
2. Listen, share, care.
3. Send encouraging notes and cards.
4. Read and discuss a book or story.
5. Make regular phone calls to encourage and say you were thinking about them.
6. Make physical contact—give hugs, shake hands.
7. Teach the person a craft or do a craft with the patient.
8. Take for a ride in the car.
9. Give hand or foot massage.
10. Play a musical instrument.
11. Show a consistent, genuine interest in that person.
12. Just spend time together.
13. Other _____
14. Other _____
15. Other _____

Spiritual Help
1. Read Bible passages aloud. (Psalms are especially good.)
2. Disciple the person.
3. Sing or provide recorded praise songs.
4. Pray with the person.
5. Share the gospel and love of Christ.
6. Pray for the person and let them know you're praying.
7. Other _____
8. Other _____

Appendix 3
What People Did to Help Mark and Shireen

As you've seen from their story, Mark and Shireen Perry were blessed with a wonderful support group of caring people. In order to help others see how they can provide that quality of support to families going through similar circumstances, Shireen has summarized here some of the things she felt were most helpful to her and to Mark.

What Helped Us
☐ *Having a great support team.* The Lord did not create us to go through life's events alone. He designed the church body to work as a team, which our church body demonstrated.

☐ *The practical, thoughtful, helpfulness of friends and family.*
Many people cleaned, shopped, ran errands, did laundry, prepared meals, and were available to do all the things Mark suggested in Appendix 2.

☐ *Being asked what we needed.*
We didn't always know, but those with experience and training could help us anticipate our needs and answer those questions.

☐ *Having others respect and help create our time together alone as a couple (especially at the very end of Mark's life).*

☐ *Laughter.*
Having and being with people who had a sense of humor was a real help.

☐ *Singing, reading and praying together.*
Especially during difficult and painful times. Music of worship and praise helped keep our focus on the Lord's presence and strength rather than the pain.

☐ *Having Mark spend his final months at home rather than in a hospital.*
This was only possible because of hospice health care and the church friends in the medical profession who filled in when hospice was short of staff.

☐ *Our church's financial, spiritual and around-the-clock prayer support.*

☐ *Having one person (Lucy Ogden) coordinate the needed resources at the end.*

☐ *A supportive pastor who became an example for others in dealing with our situation.*

What Helped Mark
Cards and notes of encouragement. Phone calls (when he was up for them). Friends bringing over lunch and eating with him. People sharing what was happening in their lives and asking him to pray for them gave him a sense of helping others. Rides to his medical appointments. Massages and hugs. Being read to from Scripture and from the biographies of Christians. Male friends in the church who prayed and counseled with him through the good and the bad times. Friends inviting us over and cooking food that conformed to the diet he was on. Shireen calling him several times a day. All the things he suggested in Appendix 2.

What Helped Shireen
Others being concerned for my needs aside from Mark's needs.

Friends making me get away from the situation for an hour or an afternoon, even though I did it reluctantly sometimes. Knowing I could call friends to pray specifically about a matter or to be a sounding board. Having a close friend and relative go with me to make the cemetery and mortuary arrangements Mark requested. Being able to let Mark die at home.

What Is Helping Shireen Now
Working on projects and dreams Mark and I shared. Having friends help me on some of those projects. Knowing the Lord Jesus is watching out for my every need, even when I feel lonely, angry or overwhelmed with responsibility. Understanding and having those around me understand the stages of grief. (I recommend these books: *Grief* by the Christian Medical Society; *Good Grief* by Granger E. Westburg; *Facing the Death of Someone You Love* by Elisabeth Elliot; and *Early Widow—A Journal of the First Year* by Mary Jane Worden.) Friends and family helping me through the anniversary dates of Mark's death (one month, six months, one year, etc.) and special days such as our wedding anniversary, birthdays and holidays. Checking on me and staying over with me in the beginning. Inviting others over for a meal helps me eat a balanced diet and not isolate myself when I'm depressed. Close friends and family who are willing to remember and talk about Mark and to cry with me when I need to cry. The freedom to ask if I can be with someone when I need company. Allowing myself to grieve at my own pace, neither running from my emotions nor getting absorbed in them. Couples continuing to include me in activities help provide some of the male perspective and interaction I miss. Knowing of people who continue to support me with prayer. Realizing it takes time to gain perspective.

Resources

General Information on AIDS:

AIDS Information Line
(U.S. Department of Health & Human Services)
800/342-AIDS

National AIDS Information Clearing House
(Centers for Disease Control)
P.O. Box 6003
Rockville, MD 20850
301/762-5111
800/458-5231

American Red Cross National
AIDS Education Program
1730 D St. N.W.
Washington, DC 20006
202/639-3223

Updates on AIDS-related ministries, education resources and public policy information:

Americans for a Sound AIDS Policy
P.O. Box 17433
Washington, DC 20041
703/471-7350

National Christian Information Center:

AIDS Crisis & Christians Today (ACCT)
P.O. Box 24647
Nashville, TN 37202-4647
615/371-1616

Christian counseling resources for AIDS and homosexuality:

Exodus International
P.O. Box 2121
San Rafael, CA 94912
415/454-1017

Love & Action 3
Church Circle #108
Annapolis, MD 21401
301/268-3442

General hospice information:

National Hospice Organization
1901 N. Moore Street
Arlington, VA 22209
703/243-5900

Locations for hospice centers and live-in settings:

Victory House
719 S.W. 4th Ct.
Ft. Lauderdale, FL 33312
305/463-0848

Local ministry that began as a result of Mark Perry's illness:

Heart to Heart Ministry
c/o First Covenant Church
455 Delores Street
San Francisco, CA 94110

City-wide cooperative ministry between evangelical churches:

Christian AIDS Council
P.O. Box 16172
San Francisco, CA 94116
(415) 255-9823

ALSO AVAILABLE FROM

InterVarsity Press
P.O. Box 1400
Downers Grove, IL 60515
1-312-964-5700

A companion videocassette, by CBN Publishing, which poignantly captures Mark's and Shireen's struggles during his illness and provides a practical model for church ministry.

35 minutes
VHS only
$19.95
ISBN 0-8308-7974-9